Lee Bell

Gaza

Also by Gloria Emerson

WINNERS AND LOSERS:
BATTLES, RETREATS, GAINS, LOSSES
AND RUINS FROM THE VIETNAM WAR
and
SOME AMERICAN MEN

Gaza

A Year in the Intifada:

A Personal Account
from an Occupied Land

GLORIA EMERSON

Published simultaneously in Canada
Printed in the United States of America

Library of Congress Cataloging-in-Publication Data

Emerson, Gloria.
    Gaza: a year in the intifada—a personal account from an
occupied land / by Gloria Emerson.
        ISBN 0-87113-445-4
        1. Gaza Strip—History—Palestinian Uprising, 1987–
—Personal narratives, American.   2. Emerson, Gloria.   I. Title.
Ds110.G3E48   1990   953'.1–dc20   90-19788

Design by Timothy O'Keeffe

The Atlantic Monthly Press
19 Union Square West
New York, NY 10003

First printing

For the parents of Tanya
and
Michael and Eleanore Kennedy

Acknowledgments

The author is particularly beholden to Joan Whitman for her wise and patient counsel and to Karen Brudney, M.D., who advised on medical details. Appreciation is also due to Hal Wyner in Israel, to H. D. S. Greenway and to the novelist Wayne Karlin, whose novel *The Extras* reveals so much about Arabs and Israelis. For their encouragement Kevin Bowen, Nicholas Cull, Peter Marin and M. J. N. Kelly have my gratitude. A particular debt is owed to Ilie Wacs, who did not endorse a book about Palestinians yet never withdrew his hospitality in New York. Matthew Kapsner and Bonnie Levy and Helaine Randerson did far more than their duties require.

Gaza was written with two women always in mind: the Israeli lawyer Tamar Peleg and the Palestinian patriot and scholar Dr. Hanan Mikhail Ashrawi, who have both taught me a new meaning of courage.

Mediterranean

Sea

GAZA STRIP

▲ Beach
▲ Jabália

● Gaza

▲ Nuseirat

▲ Bureij
Deir
el-
Balah
▲ Maghazi

ISRAEL

Khan
Younis
▲
●
Khan
Younis

▲ Refugee camps

▲ Rafah
● Rafah

Kms.
0 ——————— 10
0 ——————— 10
Miles

—·—·— Boundary of former Palestine Mandate

————— Armistice Demarcation Lines, 1949
(shown where at variance with
Mandate boundary)

··········· International boundary

Territories occupied by Israel
since 1967

Area of United Nations Disengagement
Observer Force (UNDOF)

Area of United Nations Interim
Force in Lebanon (UNIFIL)

AUDI

RABIA

©A·Karl/J·Kemp, 1991

Contents

Prelude

It is written that on the ancient road that ran along the Palestinian coast Gaza was once the last metropolis for travelers crossing the desert to Egypt and the first Palestinian city to be reached on the journey back. In the *Encyclopedia Judaica* Gaza is described as the city where, as told in the Book of Judges, Samson performed his famous deeds and perished. In the *Encyclopedia of Islam* Gaza is described as a rich city often visited by merchants from Mecca and where, in one of his journeys, the great-grandfather of Mohammed the Prophet is said to have died. Even today many Gazans believe this. Because of its crucial location Gaza was often dominated by foreign rulers and during the Roman Empire it was a prosperous and vibrant seaport. The Philistines were the first Palestinians and some scholars have noted that when Alexander the Great advanced along the coastal road to conquer Egypt Gaza was able to resist his army for five months, 332 B.C. In his history of Gaza in the early sixth century A.D. Glanville Downey quotes the pilgrim to the Holy Land who passed through in 570 A.D. and wrote in Latin: "Gaza is a splendid city, full of pleasant things; the men in it are most honest, distinguished by every generosity, and warm friends of visitors."

During the occupation of Palestine by the Turks from 1516 Gaza was briefly occupied by Napoleon in 1799 in his failed effort to possess Egypt and Syria. After the defeat of the Ottoman Empire in World War I, the Sykes-Picot Agreement drawn up by France, Britain and Russia for their own imperial gain gave Britain control over Palestine; her mandate lasted from 1920 to 1948, the imposition of an alien rule upon an unwilling people. The efforts of fearful and agitated Arabs to stop Jewish immigration and the purchase and expropriation of Palestinian land were doomed. The rise of the Third Reich gave Jewish emigration a desperate push.

On November 29, 1947, the United Nations General Assembly passed a resolution recommending the partition of Palestine into a Jewish state and a Palestinian state with an economic union between them. It was an intolerable idea for Palestinians, who would lose much of their citrus groves, grain fields and industry as well as Jaffa, the major Palestinian port on the Mediterranean. They refused and so lost everything for the state of Israel was born in May 1948. Palestine was destroyed, its people dispersed, its history forbidden and denied by the victors. In that same year Jordan occupied the West

Bank and Egypt the Gaza Strip. President Gamal Abdel Nasser, the ardent and eloquent advocate of Pan-Arabism, encouraged Palestinian attacks in Israel by guerrillas from Gaza while imposing other restrictions on their political movements. Despite some of the injustices of Egyptian rule in Gaza, Palestinians living there today remember that the Egyptians seized none of their land and enabled Gazans to study free at Egyptian universities. Nasser, most of all among the middle-aged, is a heroic memory. The P.L.O. was established as a cohesive group in 1964, its single imperative goal the liberation of Palestine rejecting the popular dogma that Arab unity was the road to the liberation of Palestine. One of the foundations of the P.L.O.'s Fatah was the belief that Palestinians should only rely on themselves, no other Arab regimes or parties could be trusted to advance their cause.

Fatah has remained the largest faction of the P.L.O. It is a mark of the peculiar and often misunderstood genius of Yasir Arafat that although under his leadership not an inch of the old Palestine has been regained he has kept alive the Palestinian cause and the longing for the homeland among a dispossessed people. And it is Arafat, considered sly and untruthful by so many in the United States, who has maintained a collective leadership keeping the various factions together under the P.L.O. roof. The Popular Front for the Liberation of Palestine is the second largest P.L.O. group, far more radical in its ideology than Fatah, followed by the Democratic Front for the Liberation of Palestine, which broke from the P.F.L.P. in 1978. Other smaller groups are in the P.L.O. family.

In 1967 Israel launched a preemptive strike against Egypt, Syria and Jordan and devastated their armies. The Six-Day War led to Israeli occupation of the Sinai Peninsula, the Golan Heights, the West Bank and Gaza. In the following years, the P.L.O. seemed indifferent to the Palestinians in the Occupied Territories finding new bases of power in Jordan and then in southern Lebanon. In 1970 King Hussein of Jordan, fearful of the threat that the P.L.O. guerrillas posed to his regime, often blatantly, struck in September and defeated Arafat's followers in a civil war for control of the kingdom. Sixty percent of Jordan's population are Palestinians. The nationalist movement in Lebanon, the strengths of the P.L.O. and their ebullient, often arrogant, behavior led to an Israeli invasion in June 1982 and Phalangist militiamen massacred hundreds of Palestinians in the Sabra and Shatila refugee camps in Beirut while Israeli forces were just outside the camps during the slaughter.

It was, as Thomas Friedman points out in *From Beirut to Jerusalem*, the Palestinians under occupation—a little under half of the four to five million Palestinians in the world—who would restore Arafat's political career and his power as a symbol, which seemed finished when he sailed out of the Beirut harbor with the remnants of his defeated followers.

The intifada began with a careless Israeli truck driver although Gazans will tell you he committed an act of revenge. Two days after an Israeli Jew, a merchant, was stabbed inside a shop for women's clothing in the Gaza marketplace an Israeli truck driver turned his semitrailer into a lane of oncoming traffic. Gazan workers in packed cars and buses were returning from work in Israel for it was 4 P.M. All the casualties—four dead Palestinians, seven others wounded—were from Jabalia Camp. As Friedman wrote in noting the rumors about the truck driver, that he wanted to avenge the murder of the Israeli or happened to be a relative: "Either way, everyone knew that when it came to Jews and Palestinians there were no accidents, only acts of war." On December 9 Palestinian youths in Jabalia threw stones at Israeli soldiers in an open truck. After the usual chase the soldiers returned to the truck, where one man had stayed behind, to find a siege under way. Shots were fired by the troops, killing seventeen-year-old Hatem Abu Sisi, whose funeral led to a furious demonstration. The following day another camp, in the Strip, rose up, then two camps in the West Bank until the entire Arab population seemed to join in. Each stone they threw was the answer to the long years when they were kept on their knees.

In a State Department report, February 1989, it was noted that the United States considers Israel's occupation to be governed by The Hague Regulations of 1907 and the 1949 Fourth Geneva Convention Relative to the Protection of Civilian Persons in Time of War. The report said: Israel denies the applicability of the Fourth Geneva Convention to the West Bank and Gaza, but states that it observes the Convention's humanitarian provisions in those areas. "Israel applies Jordanian law in the West Bank and British mandate law in Gaza," the report said, "as well as its own military orders which have changed these laws significantly."

Almost a year after the intifada began Palestine was

declared an independent state in Algiers in November
1988 by its parliament in exile. In December Chairman
Arafat made the historic concessions in the language
American diplomats required. On behalf of the Palestine National Council he accepted two states, a Palestinian state and a Jewish state, Israel. He accepted the
United Nations Security Council Resolutions 242 and
338 as the basis for negotiations and renounced all forms
of terrorism. The United States said it would hold talks
with P.L.O. representatives but the government of Israel, unmoved, refused any such contact.

After that fateful December in Gaza the old Palestinian tragedy once more rose before the world and not
only other Arabs felt engaged. Efforts were made to
persuade Americans and Israelis that the retention of
the Occupied Territories was not vital for the security
of Israel and that the real danger would be continued
occupation and "colonization." The mayor of Tel Aviv
said Israel should talk to the P.L.O. Groups in Israel
called for an end to occupation and a member of the
Knesset, Shulamit Aloni, head of the Citizens Rights
Movement, wrote: "It is universally recognized that
Palestine-Eretz Israel is the land of two peoples. The
United Nations determined this in Resolution 181 of
Nov. 29, 1947 which called for partition of the land and
was the basis for Israel's establishment. . . . It is universally recognized that Israel's borders lie within the
Green Line, i.e. the 1949 Armistice lines. This is inher-
ent in Resolutions 242 and 338, now also recognized by
the P.L.O." A former Israeli Foreign Minister, Abba
Eban, speaking at the Woodrow Wilson School at

Princeton University, said that the Israeli occupation is "the worst of all possible options from the viewpoint of logistical security." Others argued and insisted that Israel was not the obstacle to peace and some American Jews felt that a double standard was being applied by the news media as to the conduct of Israel which was unbalanced and biased.

This small book, a record of the life of Gazans for only one year, was not written in the hope of denigrating the Jewish state, only to illuminate, as so many others have done, why there is a revolution that will persist for years until the Palestinians have their nation. An American correspondent in Israel for European publications, Hal Wyner, wrote of seeing a poster from the early 1980s in a Tel Aviv bookstore that showed a photograph of an Israeli soldier beating a Palestinian. In Hebrew the poster said: "Don't say you didn't know."

In a piece published on the Op-Ed page of *The New York Times* in October 1989 Mr. Wyner wrote: "As difficult as it may be to believe, most stories on the intifada that appear in the Western media are characterized not by exaggeration but by understatement. In spite of this many non-Jewish correspondents have had to deal with accusations of anti-Semitism, while Jewish journalists (myself included) are censured for self-hatred." Mr. Wyner wrote that people who feel a hatred of Jews do so generally on the basis of long-standing prejudices and not because of anything the Jews do or do not do.

"Since anti-Semitism has its roots not in the truth

but in distortions of the truth I do not see how I can do a service to the Jewish people by concealing or distorting the truth when it comes to Israel," he wrote. ". . . The issue is not self-hatred but self-respect."

I

The Hotel, 1989

IN APRIL THAT YEAR THERE WERE MANY PEOPLE keeping count: the dead, the gunshot wounds, the beatings, the arrests, the deportations and how many schools were shut because the children charged the soldiers waiting for them outside the classrooms. Even the youngest threw stones, hopping and dancing back and forth, fingers up in a V for victory, until the Israeli troops slammed into them hard. The soldiers looked like high school boys who did not yet have children of their own. Each week more statistics flew out of this tiny place called the Gaza Strip, a rectangular slice of land not more than twenty-eight miles long and barely five miles wide, on the Mediterranean Sea. As that month in 1989 burned on the count kept rising: more than one thousand six hundred casualties just for those thirty days.

No insurrection ever yielded such constant calculations: civilian casualties, curfews, demolition of houses and even the ages of the children who were hurt. In Jerusalem and in Washington, D.C., human rights groups worked on the tallies. In Vienna and in London people saw the figures. In Tel Aviv and in Chicago, Los Angeles and Cambridge more human rights groups were keeping accounts.

The children of the town named Gaza, with its two large refugee camps, and the children living on the Strip, where six others were located, were too audacious for their own good.

In those crowded camps, in the neighborhoods in town, the children often massed when the enemy, on patrol or in jeeps, suddenly came close. Boys whistled to alert the ranks. Any number of Israelis, even a dozen, were always seen as a deliberate provocation although there were always lulls in the hostilities. Many Israelis, and Americans too, claimed that Palestinian parents forced their children to be belligerent but the young did not need to be coaxed or tutored. All that they saw in their daily lives was reason enough and it was the children who were most eager for revenge as if the matter was up to them. Many parents, who loathed the Israeli occupation, were pleased by the children's defiance but could not have kept them docile in any case; warnings went unheeded. The children believed they grew wings and would be too fast for the bullet, the club or the soldier giving chase. When caught, only the smallest were seen to be crying.

That April, in the seventeenth month of the intifada, or uprising, three children died. Six hundred and thirty-seven were injured and, among them, one hundred and forty-four were shot by live rounds. The United Nations Relief and Works Agency, which had been keeping the Palestinian refugees alive for thirty-nine years, kept that count very precisely. In the youngest age group, one to five years old, eighteen boys were beaten and five girls. The Israeli Defense Forces, in one way or another, said it was the fault of the children, some soldiers said they had it coming.

"Of course they always put the blame on us. They are so obstinate," said Ahmad Hillis, Field Education Officer at UNRWA, which ran one hundred and forty-seven elementary and preparatory schools. "I said to this officer: 'You have your arms and submachine guns, how do you expect the children not to be provoked when they see you and the military vehicles outside?' Some little girls threw stones at a jeep outside a Gaza elementary school. They were very small. But the school was closed until further notice."

How much harm could a six-year-old girl do, he asked aloud. Then he went on repeating what he had said to the Israeli colonel as if such repetition restored him: "*You* push them into the streets. If you helped them stay in school they would be too busy." And then: "When there are incidents of course the children cannot concentrate." His own statistics on how many of the schools for some eighty-nine thousand pupils had been closed for as long as three months made his face droop. In happier times he might have been free to speak of his lifelong interest in American literature, the weeks he spent at the University of Leeds in England, or ask about the new biography of Hemingway. But the intifada swallowed all other subjects, no one ever moved a foot from it, and now Mr. Hillis wanted it known how much tear gas had been used earlier that year in the Khan Younis Camp, on the Strip, after some boys acted up. They retreated into the camp, which was so heavily soaked in tear gas fifty children had to be hospitalized. It always felled the youngest and the most elderly. In April UNRWA figured that eighty-nine children suffered from exposure to it and needed medical treatment. Most Palestinians were used to it by now but a few very old women, with bad lungs, told me they saw it as a hex, a new death.

The Israelis said they had the upper hand and did not bother with a hearts-and-minds program, in the American manner, to placate and win over the Arabs for it was far too late for that. When the clashes grew too frequent, when the Gazans appeared too defiant before the troops, there was a simple response: curfew. There were two kinds: a total curfew and a partial one, applying only to a specific area inside a camp or a town. During the first year of the intifada, from December 9, 1987 to December 31, 1988, Jabalia Camp was under curfew for a total of one hundred and forty-five days, Beach Camp for one hundred and forty-nine days, in the Strip the Bureij Camp for one hundred and seventeen days and in the town of Gaza itself, the Sheikh Radwan area for fifty-three days. No one could leave their homes for any reason. Such collective punishment was poorly tolerated by Gazans and widely criticized so curfews were less frequently imposed in 1989: Jabalia Camp a total of seventy-eight days, Beach Camp a total of eighty-seven days. In the Strip the Shaboura area of the Rafah refugee camp, with twenty-five thousand people, or half the size of the entire camp, was regularly isolated with thirty-eight days of curfew plus the one hundred and ten days applied to the entire camp.

The Palestinians were penned in like barnyard animals. Only ambulances of the Red Crescent Society, the Arab Red Cross, vehicles from the hospitals or the U.N. cars were allowed in the streets. No Palestinian could do business, buy food, go to work, send the children to school, visit a relative, seek help for the sick or so much as move a few feet outside the door. People grew accustomed but hated it. It was as though a heavy curtain of lead blocked them from the world. The children, confined to such crowded rooms in the camps, grew cranky and naughty. No one ever knew how long a curfew would last. Late at night an Israeli voice on a bullhorn would announce that a curfew had begun "until further notice" or the radio would announce the bad news.

Sometimes the tear gas would seep into rooms at night and startle sleeping people with its sting. And it was the tear gas made in Pennsylvania that was killing the huge ficus tree in the garden of Marna House, the famous little hotel in town. The Palestinian gardener, summoned to diagnose the sickly tree which was dropping all its leaves despite the sweet weather, said so. Drastic surgery of all the branches began. The hotel, with its sixteen rooms and one telephone for guests on the ground floor, pulled in all the foreign delegations and the journalists. A more modern hotel, the Clift, was right on the sea but no one ever knew whether it was half-open or shut and meals were not served. Next to it, the Love Boat, Gaza's grandest restaurant and banquet hall, was where the fanciest, biggest wedding receptions were once held but it was out of business. People remembered the huge parties there, how they used to entertain each other at home, how the town buzzed and hummed with life but those days were gone for good out of respect for the grief and the losses that were covering Gaza like scales. And there was a curfew every night at eight P.M., too, so every evening people scuttled back home and stayed put.

The tree was one of three immense ficuses with double entwined trunks in the long walled garden facing Marna House, its greatest charm. A few foreigners did not want to see the branches hacked off as if the mutilated tree might be an omen. People always expected Gaza to be a dry coarse hopeless place and were startled to discover so many lush gardens, with orange trees and blossoming bushes, outside even the small villas. None was more charming than the flower beds and shrubbery of Marna House rimming a long rectangle of very green grass and the driveway. There were roses and lilies, lark-spur, huge marigolds, tall and fluffy gladioli, snapdragons and narcissus. There were palm trees which did not look upset by the tear gas and the other ficuses were doing well. But the verdict was accepted.

The garden was calming. No one went out for an aimless walk in the old pale walled city which in the sixth century A.D. had been a great Mediterranean port, a center for pottery and wine. Now it was only a name for trouble. To make army vehicles detour boys set tires on fire in the streets. Barricades went up, came down. Ev-erywhere the walls sang with commands, instructions, exhortations. The soldiers ordered any man they saw to cover the seditious walls with a whitewash he had to provide, and then watched. Anyone was conscripted. The photographs of Yasir Arafat also had to be ex-punged but his face came back in posters pasted every-where. Men were also made to remove the Palestine flags that hung from telephone wires and were not per-mitted to grumble or shirk. The Israeli Defense Forces did their own mural on a long street, covering the steel shutters of shops and the high walls with immense XXXX's in black paint as if the town were to be con-demned and this was the mark. It was strangely sinister. One soldier painted giant dollar signs on his stretch of wall, perhaps wanting to be witty or to remind the Ga-zans of the American money that went to Israel, the dear ally.

But in the garden there was a semblance of peace.

"Yes, imagine, tear gas," said Mrs. Malika Kourchid when people asked about the amputated tree. Tear gas in the garden: the pursed mouth, the raised little eyebrows, the tiny toss of the head were signals of scorn that she may have learned from a French mother. She was the owner of Marna House, who came from Beirut every year to stay in Gaza a few months; her family once lived in the house next door to the hotel. But people always thought of Marna House as belonging to her cousin, Alya Shawa, who ran the place, who knew all the journalists and how to accommodate the visiting foreign delegations who wanted an experience. She knew everything.

Alya Shawa did not care about the ruined tree. The intifada had nothing to do with trees and in the spring she looked pale and deeply troubled. It was thought that her headaches were back but she never spoke of it. Every day Mrs. Shawa, whose large family was once among the richest property owners in Gaza, found out what was going on. There were her couriers and the telephone calls and the invisible communiqués that wafted into her small office with its old brown forbidden map of Palestine. Marna House was her domain.

April and May were deathly. The Israelis kept very busy.

"Every time someone is shot then Alya is shot," said Mrs. Kourchid, who kept fussing about the garden, offended by weeds or a disobedient shrub, and often went into the huge dark kitchen, which lacked a single useful appliance, to cook so she would not have to think about the bombings in Beirut. Sometimes Malika sewed while Alya knitted, spoke on the telephone, wrote out bills for

guests or planned the meals. Both of them spoke English
very well, as all Shawas did, and rarely went out since
Gaza, where they grew up, was now such a different
place, the sight of the soldiers so offensive to them.
Years ago, living in Beirut where she raised her son, Alya
had once fussed about hairdressers and haute couture,
liked big parties and gambling, but since the intifada
every flutter of the old frivolity had disappeared. She
only cared about the intifada and would not even put
flowers in the living room. Her only distraction was in
the afternoon watching a soap opera from Cairo on the
television. Many foreigners saw the old traces of beauty
in that face with the slow little smile, the high and broad
cheekbones, the dark melancholic eyes and often took
her picture.

Once that spring, wanting to cheer her up, an
American showed Alya a page from a small newspaper
in New Jersey which listed all the names of the Palestinians killed during the intifada the year before.

"What good does that do us here?" she said very
softly.

There were rules at Marna House and no one broke
Alya's rules: no weapons on the premises were allowed,
no Palestinian on the run could hide here, hard liquor
was not served although people did drink in their rooms,
and no women were to be taken upstairs. Marna House
was a respectable place, everyone thought so.

The Palestinians also knew the hotel was a safe place
to talk to foreigners who wanted to hear their stories, to
meet the delegations who wanted to be led through the
camps. The army rarely came barging in. Alya Shawa
was too famous in the Occupied Territories, she had

helped too many journalists, put up too many European and American television crews and makers of documentaries so that a legion of well-placed friends would hold the Israelis to account if she was bullied or disturbed. Only twice had soldiers ever entered the grounds and met with her regal contempt and profound disdain.

In the happy garden, where the wild cats leapt on the rattan chairs, some men in Gaza spread out their lives for you as though they were bloodied torn banners of an old regiment and meant much more than a single story. What was surprising was how many Palestinians were willing to talk, give names and dates and facts and political allegiances, without being sure of how these disclosures would be used. They were oddly trusting in a place that was crawling with Shin Bet, the Israeli domestic intelligence agency, and informers. But if one Gazan trusted you then others would.

It was often startling to take notes and get all the violent details straight.

"Can you describe this metal bar in the Gaza jail—"

"The bar was about five centimeters away from the wall. Your wrists are tied to the bar which is low so your knees are bending. A sack is over your head and you are without clothes."

It was Khaled speaking, a thirty-one-year-old Gazan with a full dark beard, a halo of curly hair and huge eyes. He often looked pained or impatient. He was a member of the Popular Front for the Liberation of Palestine. His real name was too well known in Gaza and the Strip even to be written down for he was known and admired everywhere, this quick generous excitable man. He wanted to make clear that a man need not be destroyed by interrogation by the Shin Bet. He needed to believe he had learned this, and much more, in 1983, 1985 and 1988 when he had been in prison. There were all these arrests and rearrests and it was assumed that he would be taken again. His English was rough but adequate and, as did many Palestinians, he used the present tense when speaking of the past.

"Okay, the main thing when we are under interrogation is how the Shin Bet wants us to think that we alone and not remembered. They want you to feel you are nothing, living in darkness, without protection. They—the Shin Bet—are representatives of the Israeli state, the strongest state, but I, a Palestinian, am so alone. A small thing opposite a very strong thing. So I have to change the battle between me and him. I have to remember I have all the Palestinian people with me so I am equal. I have a belief but he is just working, a job. So this gives me power and imagination."

He was forced to kneel during the early interrogation and was handcuffed. When the beatings made it impossible to stand his hands were tied to the bar. He heard screaming and crying, it did not only come from him.

"How we struggle inside interrogation! I felt I might be going crazy so I began shouting. The Shin Bet officer speaks to me: 'You are going to go crazy here, you will lose everything, you are destroying your future.' I was trying only to get a main idea for the reply. 'I'd love to be crazy, this is my hope in life. If I am going to go crazy I'll be the most respected. I will be very respected by my people.'"

"No, you are stupid. People are laughing at you,"

the Shin Bet man said to Khaled. But the suffering man knew better. At one moment Khaled thought he was making an interrogator nervous so that helped him rally. They threatened, they wheedled but still he would not abdicate although he was going slightly mad, a relief of sorts.

"They said: 'Your wife has no ID card so we are going to deport her.' I told them: 'Yes, do it for me. You will be doing me a favor, I don't know her very well and you will give me a chance.' " By talking he hoped to pull them down.

His wife was a foreigner who was perfectly happy to live like any Gazan and her Arabic was good. The couple had a small son whom Khaled adored although he had wanted a daughter, not a son who might have a life like his.

"I never imagined that I could last without sleep for seven to eight days. I realized that I have something inside myself that every human being has, the power and energy to survive in a very, very bad situation. So this gave me the happiest moments of my life inside interrogation.

"I have to pretend nothing affects me. They bring me a mirror and to look in it is horrible. What I see is not my face. Not mine. I am thinking of death, death is a victory. Death for them is a disappointment, every secret of the Popular Front is gone."

His was an interesting life for the child who was born to be rich. The father, a well-to-do merchant who owned a small orange grove, traveled to Egypt on business and was never allowed by the Israelis to return. His mother opened a shop and did not permit anyone to pity them.

"I was lucky to have a strong mother, she loves me and she respects me. After the death of Che Guevara Gaza"—he referred to a leader of the Popular Front—"the phenomenon of armed struggle was finished. It was a time of hopeless depression, horrible times, from 1972 to 1977, I tried to find my way in life. I wanted to have a theory in my life." He meant a cause, a struggle, a braver and more important path.

He went to Egypt to be with his father, he studied at Bir Zeit University in Ramallah on the West Bank, he flirted with foreign girls because he knew they would always leave to go back home. The epiphany came, by chance, reading the Palestinian writer Ghassan Kanafani, and others in exile.

"I read a short story 'Letter from Gaza,' I read it ten times, my eyes were full of tears and it led me to decide to return home and struggle. No one argued with me. I came back in 1979." He became the head of the large family, taking the place of the exiled father, holding all the relatives in his wide serious embrace and keeping the children steadfast. His own mother was known as a passionate supporter of the P.L.O.

An American friend of Khaled always thought that he might be killed. A Palestinian friend said it would be safer for him back in prison. Others felt that the Israelis would not kill him because it would cause too much of an uproar and it was not worth such a commotion. He was not dangerous because he was guarding a weapons cache, or planning an attack, although he knew every murmur inside the resistance, every group, every set-back, and exactly who was where. His face gave him away, it was not ordinary enough but too fiercely lit. He was a menace because he was so widely known and admired. There was nowhere in Gaza he could go without finding friends.

Khaled was careless with himself. Often an act of kindness put him in danger; one night he was late in getting home because he was pushing a stalled car when it was nearly curfew. A patrol was out and might have opened fire, the soldiers could make up their own scenario for any death. The nervous man always grew calm in such moments and sometimes was lucky. He was able to get home in the dark just in time. Many young men chose not to be too cautious as if this habit might diminish them. Khaled would never check his car for hidden explosives or stay inside on the more dangerous days.

"I don't like to hide myself. They can do what they want," Khaled said. He was a man of immense, often wasteful, energy but talking so much in English that day had worn him down a little for the war with the interrogators was still being fought inside his brain, the terrible and uneven match. His trouble was that although he did not wish for it Khaled did not deeply fear death anymore. Being killed seemed to the unhappy man a way of finally having the last word.

Of course he was guilty of helping the Gazans to thwart or mock the occupation. All Gazans were guilty, they were a stubborn and mutinous people and the Israelis knew as much. The entire population, believed to be around seven hundred thousand since a census had not been done for decades, were always scheming to defy the

Israeli Defense Forces, the Civil Administration, an arm
of the military which ran the region, the Border Police,
the tax inspectors. The merchants shut their shops at
noon in honor of the intifada. Men did not go to work
in Israel when a general strike was called by Unified
Leadership, the underground cell in Jerusalem, which
spoke in a great baritone to the people through its numbered leaflets sent on a fax machine. Unified Leadership
had directions for everyone on how to lead their lives
and how to oppose the occupiers. *Education is part of
our struggle,* said one leaflet, number forty-five, four
pages long. *Therefore the UNL calls on our students to
concentrate during their school hours and to differentiate
between this part of the struggle and other nationalistic
activities that they carry out after school hours.* The father's voice was often stern: *The UNL calls on our
people to adhere to strike days and keep its sanctity and
not to go on picnics these days.* There was the boycott
of all Israeli products. There was an underground of
little shops that people ran in their homes when they
could find or grow things to sell and a few tiny factories
too. A private blood bank was open in town so people
never had to go to Shifa Hospital and although it was
an alien idea in their culture, men were glad to give. No
one knew the numbers of how many Gazan men refused
to go on working in Israel because they had never signed
up in the government-run work offices. But every day
you met some men in the camps who had given up their
old jobs in Israel and were so much worse off even if their
pay had once been wretched, the jobs always the most
lowly.

There were nineteen Israeli settlements in Gaza and

the Strip, on more than thirty percent of the land. Unlike the West Bank where Israeli settlers were fond of hiking in groups over the holy terrain no Jews living here went on such walks. This was not the Biblical land of their people and Arabs were too close. Although none of the settlements had ever been attacked, Israeli soldiers always guarded them. So the Jewish inhabitants were almost never seen, except in cars going one way to Beersheba, another to Tel Aviv.

A few Israeli civilians came to Gaza but even the most thick-skinned and indifferent did not feel at ease. The Israeli camera crews from the American networks, based in Tel Aviv, came on reconnaissance but were often stymied and went home without film. Boys stoned their cars with the hated yellow license plates, the giveaway, and when some men covered the plates the cars were stoned anyway. If the crews tried to film clashes the Israelis sealed off the area and gave them one warning to get out. A jeep with a snow shovel device in front pushed a car out if the driver was too slow. Officers in the Israeli Defense Forces, or I.D.F., had their orders never to permit journalists to work while a confrontation was going on—too much had already been filmed and recorded—and showed no leniency to Israeli crews. The army gave the impression that the journalists had already been too much help to the intifada.

The networks all had scanners in their cars so they could listen to the Israeli military radio and find out fast where the trouble was. They put shatterproof glass in all the windows of the rented cars. Many of the Israeli crews stopped going into the camps that year for feelings were running too high and no one ever tried to tell them it was safe in Jabalia, safe in Beach Camp or in Rafah. If the American correspondent was with them, they had no choice but never relished it.

A CBS soundman, one of the best, had a tiny secret that he did not tell his colleagues, who might have laughed. He was mobilized for the Six-Day War in 1967 when all men were called up for the perilous hour at hand. The Six-Day War ended with a victory when the Israelis annexed the Sinai Peninsula, the Golan Heights, the West Bank and Gaza. His unit drove through Gaza when the Egyptians were routed and everything was theirs. The jubilant troops, so pleased with themselves, hardly saw the faces of the Palestinians, who watched in silence, the sadness so deep that it filled their chests like a poison gas. (Afterward Graham Greene remembered the white flags still dangling from many houses in Gaza.)

"I'm so ashamed to think of it now," Schlomo said, cruising around the town. "I kept flashing the V for victory sign at them, over and over. I didn't know any better."

On all the numerous anniversaries so loved and needed by the Palestinians—Land Day to protest Israeli expropriation of land or the founding of Fatah—the troops increased their sweeps and the journalists often came back. In the spring an Israeli reporter from *The Jerusalem Post* called to make a reservation at Marna House for one night. Alya, who checked the woman out and was told she was okay, knew her duty. Facing guests she did not want or like she always stayed serene but distant, as if royal blood had taught her how to rise very far above it. Sometimes she wore her long embroidered Palestinian black dress, the next best thing to showing the flag.

At the long table in the dining room, always so nicely set, the guests ate dinner together at seven P.M. or earlier if they could so the cook might make it home on his bicycle before curfew. No one spoke much that night except to say, as people said every night, how very good the fish or chicken was, how marvelous the grapes and apples, the lemons and tomatoes. Most guests ate better at Marna House than at home in their own countries, the food so much fresher.

The presence of an Israeli made people uneasy, she saw that soon enough and did not let it matter. There was nothing offensive about her, the long sharp face looked intelligent and tired. Her English was excellent and she wrote the daily dispatches about the confrontations, killings and arrests in Gaza and the Strip, using official and Palestinian sources since their numbers were never the same. But she possessed a slight hauteur, a barely concealed sense of her own superiority that was not easy to admire but so did some Americans. Alya always watched the guests being seated, sometimes explaining the different dishes, then ate pita bread and soft cheese from a plate, in her favorite old armchair in the living room, watching television. She always needed a bit of peace.

It was the first anniversary of the death of Abu Jihad, second in command to Chairman Yasir Arafat. His uncle still had a house in Gaza where the P.L.O. leader, born Khalil el-Wazir, spent part of his childhood. An article in *The Washington Monthly* by Daniel

Halevy and Neil Livingstone describing the assassination made clear how Israel needed to prove that it could carry out such a secret and bold military operation abroad at a time when their own military forces had been so stained by the 1982 invasion of Lebanon, and again by the confusion and brutality widely seen on television in the first months of the uprising. The army's prestige was suffering. And the Israelis also thought that Abu Jihad was directing the insurrection in the territories and was long considered to have been the architect and commander of many P.L.O. military operations which killed Israelis. They considered him superior to Arafat, the writers said, because of his "shrewdness, his intelligence and operational experience." It was also noted that Abu Jihad read *The Jerusalem Post* every day and when the war was won intended to learn Hebrew.

He was asleep in his home in a Tunis suburb when one of the specially trained Israeli commandos entered the bedroom and used a silenced submachine gun, his marksmanship so perfect that the wife next to the slain man was not hurt by intent. The cruel perfect choreography of it brought joy to the generals, the public, the planners and the politicians.

When dinner was finished the night the Israeli reporter arrived, all of us out in the garden again, she wanted to take a walk but the six people with the BBC unit refused. There was still work to do and the cameramen could hardly film at night.

So the two of us walked around the corner to Shifa Hospital where there was the glare of fluorescent lights in the wards all night and the restless male patients, able to stand or hobble, looking out of the windows on the second floor which never had screens. The women were in wards on a lower floor and stayed in their beds.

Because it was a government hospital, it was forbidden for reporters to enter without authorization, rarely granted, and question patients or the staff, who would be penalized for speaking to them. Journalists did, anyway, usually at night, roaming the two floors with their overflowing toilets, the grimy walls, the operating rooms still not cleaned long after surgery, and the skeletal, starved cats that went where they pleased. The patients were always glad to see foreign journalists and kept a lookout.

The reporter, who spoke Arabic, entered Shifa Hospital as if access was normal and no one would question her presence. She asked to see a list of patients admitted that day. The fat weary Palestinian on duty, whose desk might have belonged to a schoolchild, did not know how to refuse her. The reporter looked at the record written by hand, all the names and all the wounds. Finished with that, she was ready to go but there were voices outside in the hall.

It was an ordinary scene, not one of great commotion. No one was on a stretcher, no one was dying, no boy so badly beaten he could not bear the weight of a sheet. A tall elderly Arab dressed as men of his age so often did in the long robe called a *galabiyeh*, and a jacket, was trying to walk, not stagger. Two younger and shorter men propelled him down the hall to the room where sutures would be done. The wound on his scalp looked as if he had been hit by a club, the kind with nails in it, and he was bleeding so much because of the vascular network in the skull. No one at the hospital came forward with a wheelchair.

It was I who wanted to follow but the Israeli said, no, she did not want to see it, she could not take that kind of thing. Walking back to Marna House, both of us making the wrong turn, she had something to say, even to a stranger. There were rules set down by the Israeli Defense Forces on what parts of the body could be struck and she knew these rules very precisely. But it was no use paying attention; the rules were only euphemisms.

"It must be so bad for the soldiers, they know what they are doing," she said, in open distress. There was not an important story in Gaza for her on the anniversary of the killing, no one could ever predict when trouble would begin. The Palestinians revolted in large numbers only after the Israelis attacked or provoked them. Almost every night, after the curfew, I would walk down to Shifa Hospital and sometimes wonder what the bright Israeli reporter might say. There were always soldiers on guard with a submachine gun posted on top of the higher unfinished structure that was to be the new hospital. Sometimes when several ambulances arrived and the wounded were taken in, the stretchers left on the ground were deeply stained with blood. The soldiers loved seeing the casualties and began to clap or whistle as if a celebration was in order.

On one warm night a young couple from Rafah were outside Shifa to go home with their infant son who had been shot. The mother sat on the curb for more than twenty minutes while the father tried to stop a

U.N. car, or any authorized vehicle, that might give them a lift. The soldiers were singing that night as drunk men sing, slurring and bawling the same chorus over and over, entranced by their own racket. The woman put her face down to the baby she held but it was the man's wracked face that was not so easily forgotten. Finally a hospital van, which took patients home, picked them up. The young male nurses, taking a break on the stairs outside admissions, did not look up at the soldiers, who could see all of us in the light. It was never certain that, even by mistake, they would not begin to pick us off perhaps only one or two. The soldiers left every night.

The curfew at eight P.M. made visitors often feel as if a lid was coming down too close to their heads. Foreigners living in the hotel became restless and were glad of a chance to get to the bar at the Beach Club on the water which was run for U.N. personnel, who could invite guests. There was a nice dining room overlooking the sea, a big sun deck, inexpensive rooms and a few U.N. officers on leave from Lebanon who took their R and R here. Journalists were barred, so were Palestinians and Israelis.

No one liked the night unless they were drinking in the Beach Club. The soldiers were jumpiest in the dark but at the same time never so free. The tailor in Beach Camp, who was thirty-five years old, was still furious about how he was wounded. "I always knew something would happen," he said but could not explain his premonition. Mohammed was still in pain from the multiple fractures in his left leg and lay on a little bed in the largest room of his cinderblock house where visitors clustered.

"I was hit by a plastic bullet at close range. I prefer a live bullet because *that* goes in and goes out. The plastic bullet spins," he said. It was wrong: the M-16 bullet tumbled, the plastic bullet which was eighty percent zinc with a plastic resin did not but caused profound damage when fired at close range.

It began with a sick child: a four-and-a-half-year-old daughter had a stomach pain and a fever. The worried father insisted she needed a doctor and that the two of them, after midnight, should go to the hospital. A neighbor saw the headlights of a Red Cross car outside so he ventured out with the girl.

"Suddenly an Israeli jeep stopped in front of me. I raised the child up with my right arm, as a sign of peace. I tried to tell him why I was out and he shot me. Five bullets," the tailor said. There was immense confusion; a woman said the soldier had tried to pick up the child who was then snatched from his arms by neighbors. The soldier kept demanding the shot man's ID card as he lay on the ground and intended to take the victim in custody. But there was a Red Cross car outside and the helpful driver, who collected the bullets and pocketed them for evidence, intervened. An ambulance finally came and took the tailor to the Ahli Arab Hospital. The girl said nothing all that night and weeks after the shooting seemed too shy. She had been frightened to death and still hid inside her own deep hole. That day the child crept into the room and sat by the father's long soiled foot sticking out of the cast.

"I can't sleep," Mohammed said. "In twenty-four hours I only sleep for two. Sometimes I take short naps." Even in Gaza his story was startling and he was not yet at the point where he could speak calmly of that night. Imprisoned three times—Mohammed was matter of fact about it as were most men who had been sent away since they were not criminals but patriots—he could still not believe the shooting. Coming home the first time from the hospital, he behaved so strangely that his soliloquies, silences and spasms of rage alarmed his wife, who had him readmitted. The leg would be in a cast for five months and was not healing properly. He needed calcium.

The greatest offense came later. A court order summoned him to answer the charge of violating curfew as if he had committed the crime. You had only to sit with Mohammed a little while before noticing that, although laying quite still for once, he was trembling slightly with rage. He wanted to sue the Israelis but was dissuaded by a lawyer in Jerusalem. He had a lot to say about the soldier who ruined his left leg.

"Of course he doesn't know me, a graduate of the Islamic University here in Gaza. And you might say, prison was another university. According to the laws that he knows, each modern state teaches ethics to its soldiers before giving them a gun." He waved away an interruption and held to his fanciful idea. "Above all according to international laws made in Geneva if the fighter raises his hand in peace, or in a surrender, the soldier has to respect this. But the Israelis are not soldiers, they are boys who only know one thing: how to be the enemy of all Palestinians."

He liked going back to the hospital clinic at Ahli Arab Hospital to see his orthopedic surgeon, Dr. Swee

Chai Ang, a young Chinese woman from Singapore who
had trained and lived in London. It touched him that
she was so patient and attentive with all the wounded.
Once she even made a house call to see him because that
leg worried her. He was a bad patient, too, restless and
imperious, forgetting to keep the cast elevated and using
the crutches too much.

Few of her patients knew that the surgeon had
worked as a volunteer in West Beirut with the victims
of the 1982 massacre in the Sabra and Shatila camps,
later awarded the Star of Palestine by Yasir Arafat for
her courage and devotion to the Palestinians. In Gaza
she was so critical of the occupation that it was hardly
a surprise when she was not permitted to extend her
stay. In Britain the woman was famous and the BBC was
making a documentary on her that spring, *Life Under
Occupation*.

"The Europeans and the Americans should know of
our suffering," Mohammed said. It never occurred to
him that Westerners would not mind. So many Palestinians did not realize that because of the killings by the
more extreme elements of the P.L.O., who were often
opposed to Arafat, that many Europeans and Americans
would be happy to hear of their ordeal. Then the wound-
up man began moving back to his favorite theme, that
despite death and starvation the Gazans would never
capitulate. But even the strongest victims can prove
wearisome if they keep telling you how they are ready
to die and some Americans, in their impatience, found
the Gazans too passive. They wanted a movement, a
clever strategy, perhaps a peace march with hundreds of

thousands of Gazans surging to Erez checkpoint where the Arabs entered Israel. But the Palestinians knew better and only smiled.

"What about the children, your little girl—would it be so easy to see her die from hunger of malnutrition?" Perhaps the interpreter put it more politely for it took some time for the question to float over to the wounded man. He thought and then said something to the child, waiting for her response.

The undersized girl, head down and hands in lap, whispered in Arabic and the answer pleased him. He gave her a long important look and said she could go play.

"She understands even at her age," the tailor said. He wanted to prepare her for the struggle if he should fail or die. But it was the nameless soldier that night in Beach Camp—maybe as scared of the dark as she was— who had taught her everything and the father must have known as much.

People repeated the wretched story, it was the stuff of all their lives, the proof of the insanity that was running rampant. Foreigners living in Gaza tended to believe that such violent acts were not deviations at all from official I.D.F. policy but permitted, if not sanctioned, by the military.

Walking near the hotel, down the street of the Shifa Hospital, was not always an easy stroll. The boys of Gaza, the shock troops, sometimes flung used canisters of tear gas on the telephone wires. MK II 560 CS 750 Yards Long Range Projectile Warning: May Start Fires Must Not Be Fired Directly At Persons As Death Or Injury May Result. Once a child with a squarish head and odd eyes handed me a canister: Federal Triple Chaser Grenade Chemical Irritating Agent (CS) May Start Fires For Outdoor Use Only. "From America," the boy said, as if he had been practicing his English. The canisters did say that: Federal Laboratories Saltzburg Penn. Made in USA.

They threw up other things on the wires too: a Palestinian flag or the rocks and stones that were their only weapons. If they needed weights anything would do: an old shoe or sandal or stick. So all these things dangled like lunatic mobiles from shreds of cloth or string.

When the neighborhood did not know the foreigner walking about it was the children in the streets who would investigate in their crude little fashion, moving in like tiny terriers. There was a simple test. "Shalom," said the girl in a soiled yellow dress, several sizes too large. It was a mistake to return the greeting but the habit was old. "Yahoud," she said, passing sentence. The word meant Jew. Two blocks away some boys were playing a good game of soccer but the vigilantes were too small for that. A passerby told the children to go away and not to throw stones. He was a man who knew I was living at Marna House; all of Gaza was covered with eyes that never blink.

In the hospital wards, the wounded children wanted to put up a good front and sometimes did, raising their fingers or making little speeches. People always went to Ahli Arab Hospital, near Palestine Square, because it was the only private hospital in Gaza and the Strip, run by the Episcopal Diocese of Jerusalem. There were only sixty-seven beds in buildings that were between seventy-five and one hundred years old inside a large compound with outpatient clinics. It was Ahli, under an agreement with UNRWA, that took patients referred by the Health Clinics in the camps. The two operating rooms were too busy, the average was two hundred sixty operations a month in 1988. There was no elevator and the children were put in wards with adults.

A ten-year-old boy lifted a sheet to show the visitor what had happened: she was the fifth foreigner that week to inquire. He had been shot in the stomach and the scar was huge. The American wanted to know if he could eat fruit or candy; the answer was no. The grown men, sitting around the next bed where a comatose man lay, heard every word and butted in. The first to speak wore the white knitted cap of the devout Muslim and had the ample well-groomed mustache of the literary British colonel. He spoke as a headmaster would to the slightly slow student.

"Food is not a present," he said. "What the present should be is a reminder of you. That's what you should bring." The child, still in pain, wished he might have kept the bullet that did him in. The man's voice grew deeper as new thoughts occurred. Gazans are not a meek people but talkative and robust; theirs is an intensely verbal culture.

"And the present should be that Americans give love to the Palestinians," he said. It was a command, the voice had now become a drum and the shot boy, who was trying to move, sought comfort by putting his face deep into the pillow. He pretended to have done something heroic but he was only shot because he loitered during a clash with troops. The older man was now dictating the letter that should be immediately sent to President Bush so he would recognize the Palestinian ordeal.

In the wards were the reminders of the years when the British fought in Palestine, the big bronze plaques that held the loving messages. "To The Memory of Capt. Ivor T. Lloyd Jones 7th Bt M.F. Born at Llandinam, Wales Feb. 10, 1895. Educated at the Leys School, Cambridge. Fell at Gaza, March 26th 1917. Jesus said unto him Follow Me and he arose and followed Him. St. Matt. 9C 9V. By his Mother. Also to the Memory of George Williams, PTE, His Faithful Servant Who Fell With Him." A ward was dedicated to the memory of his parents by their son, Captain G. A. Schofield, November 1917. There had been fighting here during World War I when the British Army in Egypt—the Egyptian Expeditionary Force—fought in Gaza because it dominated the coastal road to Palestine. The enemies were the Turks of the Ottoman Empire and their German commanders.

Still bitter at the British for the Balfour Declaration of 1917 pledging British support for a Jewish National Home in Palestine no one had ever defaced the plaques or ripped them down. No one even saw them anymore.

People who thought of all Arabs as dirty were surprised by the cleanliness of the wards, the clinics and even the cramped little emergency room. In comparison Shifa Hospital was a giant abscess; patients at Ahli often had to be transferred there and were not pleased. Too many microbes here, as one of the male nurses at Shifa said. Inside the large compound of Ahli Arab Hospital was the Baptist Nursing School where forty-one men and women studied for three years in English, their classes and homework demanding nine to ten hours a day. The American who ran the school thought some of the flowers growing in the compound, or on the Strip, reminded him of his native Arkansas. "The daisies, the bougainvillea, the nasturtiums, the sweet peas, the ferns and hibiscus," said Karl Weathers, an amiable and dedicated man with a nice bit of pink in his complexion. It was pleasant to talk about the flowers that he was showing me instead of immediately asking if amoebic dysentery was common in the camps. It was. There was typhoid once in a while, he said, because of the filth and open sewers in the camps. An American doctor at Ahli was surprised by the numbers of men with peptic ulcers, which in the States had almost disappeared.

"It depends on the day," Mr. Weathers said, of typhoid or various ailments or maybe meaning something larger.

Not all the foreigners in the delegations were upset by the sight of the many wounded children after touring Ahli Arab Hospital. "These kids didn't look very *pacifistic* to me," said one American, back in the garden, with the delegation assembled by the intelligent, pleasant wife of a U.S. Senator. A very tall man—slightly too well-dressed for such a trip, and clearly accustomed to having his say—he wanted to talk about Yad Vashem, the hilltop memorial in Jerusalem honoring the six million Jews killed in the Holocaust that he had just visited. He expected the rest of us to hear what the guide there had said, how no help had been given these doomed murdered Jews, as if the others might not know. On a small, hidden level he seemed to be saying that Jews had never known mercy and nothing he had seen in Gaza called up for mercy in him.

"Yes to death and starvation," said the huge sign condemning the occupation, which was written in Arabic on the back of the building that was Shifa Hospital. It stayed there for months. On some days, when the pandemonium was at a lower level, numerous men found time to explain what a dark light fell on them, how the Israelis were pulling the garrote tighter around their necks. Everyone talked about money, which meant the swollen and huge taxes leveled by the occupiers. More than one Gazan said outright that Gazans were paying for the occupation and it was hard to argue with that.

But starvation was far away in the Sudan and the Sahel, it did not seem possible to starve in Gaza. On the Strip, a shallow fertile valley between sand dunes on the west and irregular hills in the south and east, huge cactus hedges hid many of the small fields and gardens. Vendors sold fresh grapes, tomatoes, lemons and watermelon by the road at low prices. You could fill your own box with the fresh green grapes that tasted sweeter than any others and only pay six shekels, or three dollars.

It shocked people seeing the Strip for the first time to realize how fertile and green it was, how lovable the land where orange trees would blossom and bear fruit at the same time. The camels were only odd compared to the computer-coded magnetic ID cards that every Palestinian going to Israel had to have. There were always the fierce, stupid contrasts of any war: herds of dark brown and white goats on the same streets as soldiers with the AR-15, with the Uzi, and the greatest swagger that any army ever chose to have.

Taxes were the oldest way of keeping a people subservient and frightened; the men in the camps who worked full time in Israel paid taxes. The worn wrinkled men whose flat open carts were pulled on tires by donkeys paid for a license plate, thirty dollars a year. Even the rich, who owned businesses or land, houses and good cars, felt the lash as deeply as anyone did. Taxes made Gazans as furious as the demolition of houses. In the office of an accountant near Marna House, a tax specialist, accustomed to calming his clients, blew up when he heard me say that Israelis paid horrible taxes, too. Others in the office were surprised to hear him shout but everyone's nerves were scraped.

"Yes but the Jews get something. What do we get? Bombs, guns, grenades, tear gas, explosives. Not new roads or municipal services. Not pickup of garbage. Nothing," he bellowed. "We pay for the occupation."

The Civil Administration, directed by Israeli civilian staff officers, governed such a wide range of Palestinian affairs it regulated most aspects of the lives of Gazans. Nearly eighty percent of their budget came from taxes and licensing fees paid by residents of the Occupied Territories.

No man had a more mournful tale than the brother of Alya, Aoun Shawa, who at fifty-five years of age was a small businessman targeted for ruin. He owned the little Shawa supermarket on Jalla Street which opened in 1970 and flourished for more than a decade. He thought the end started when the right-wing party of

Yitzhak Shamir, the Likud, came to power early in the decade. Walking around the store with its emptied shelves and vacant freezers, Mr. Shawa remembered what had once been his pride. Every space told him what was missing.

"This was full of all kinds of soups: mushroom, onion, pea, tomato and chicken. There were dried soups, too. Oh I have seen my shop deteriorating," he said. Once he sold twenty bottles of ketchup a week because people liked to put it on chips and meat, Mr. Shawa said, but because of the boycott on Israeli products he did not order it anymore.

"I can't get Arabic ketchup," he explained. There were a few imported luxuries left: four jars of Heinz Hamburger Relish and three bottles of Kraft French Dressing. Mayonnaise from Israel cost too much so he had sold jars of it from Belgium but that was finished, too. Salt, flour, sugar and ground coconut all came from Israel, there was no other resource.

"When Likud came to power in the nineteen eighties things started to get tough. The philosophy of Likud was to make it harder for Palestinians to survive. They would prefer us to disappear. Yes, the population has suffered economically from the intifada, purchasing power has declined and jobs were lost or given up. We accept the way things are going, the intifada should go on. We have no other way."

A customer came in for cream but there was none. Two people bought bottled water, a third a pack of Marlboro cigarettes. A woman bought a package of frozen okra. Mr. Shawa said an ordinary television set would now cost between twelve hundred and fifteen hundred dollars as there was a tax of three hundred percent on such an item.

He spoke wistfully of what had been plentiful in the Shawa supermarket: Camembert and Gruyère cheese from France, appliances from Japan and gadgets too, pots from France and Taiwan, boxes of California rice, chocolates and toffee from Britain, cookies from Denmark. Peanut butter had not been a success, Arabs did not like it.

"In taxes I lose fifty percent of my profits," he said, walking by the shelf with cereals and Arab macaroni. "The weakness lies not in the regulations but in its application and enforcement which is arbitrary and, of course, arrogant."

A man bought a copy of *The Jerusalem Post*. Alya's son, Mohammed, was at the cash register with nothing much to do.

"There is no room for discussion or appeal. You cannot discuss your income tax. I am always confronted by tax people who ask for sums of money that I have never, never earned, more than I have earned," said Mr. Shawa. Once he had sold cold cuts, dried meat and less expensive cuts of veal, lamb or turkey.

"Deserted," he said, looking into the freezer that was just for meat.

In his tiny office in back, he sat with a hand propping his thin, handsome, troubled face.

"Since the intifada there are only Israelis in the tax department, in customs, there are no Gazans, who all quit. So the Israelis come with their machine guns, not as respectable government employees," he said in his

low knotted voice. No one came in the very clean modern little store which had once been so crowded.

"All Israelis are soldiers, in uniforms or not. And
they say: 'You have made such and such a mistake and
you owe such and such.' If I say they are mistaken they
will confiscate the store. They bullied me terribly in
August 1987—four or five men jumping out of a jeep
and one car, *civilians with machine guns,* charging into
this office, taking all my papers, saying 'Come with us.' "
In the customs department of the Civil Administration
he was forced to pay twelve thousand dollars. The dispute was over the amount due for Value Added Tax, or
VAT, which is fifteen percent of the price of imported
goods. It is passed on to the customer but Mr. Shawa
was accused of withholding it.

There were once ten employees in the supermarket
but now there were only three. He made sure that I
understood all the prohibitions clamped on Gazans: no
Palestine flag, no national anthem, no peace sign. And
then: no recourse when Israelis took your ID card away,
no purchase of any land without permission and no right
to sell without permission, no meetings of more than five
men although an exception was made for the august
members of the Benevolent Society of Gaza because
they were notables. But even a notable could not open
a new office without permission. The paperwork and the
lost time were incalculable.

He felt like a hunted man. Owing taxes he was
fearful of getting the new license for his car which would
not be renewed if he had not paid up. Stamps were
pasted on the windshield as proof all accounts were paid.

The supermarket was not an asset anymore but there were still the ten acres of land on which he grew tomatoes, not citrus as so many others did. The taxes on agricultural products were not heavy but there were other problems. Farmers were not allowed to import any citrus or vegetables that would compete with the Israeli market. Prices were too low in Gaza because the Israelis often dumped their own surpluses on the market driving the price down.

"Only this season we were able to export some things to Holland. A shipment to Norway of Gaza vegetables goes next week. I have a greenhouse for the tomatoes and an open field for green peppers and a chicken farm for eggs—seven workers. Farm products are never that profitable, I started to build a house but couldn't keep on with it."

Several factors had hurt the Palestinians in recent years, Mr. Shawa said, standing up now by the shelf with cans of fava beans from Jerusalem. The behavior of the rulers of the Gulf States, their extravagance and corruption, were deplorable. An era of "terrorism," he added, had not achieved anything.

"Some Palestinian organizations thought it wise to act against civilian targets in the West. I doubt this has served us well. With all the killings by Islamic extremists—it has hurt a lot.

"It's such an old story—two adversaries. The other man's thumb in our mouth so we start biting. Whoever can endure will be the winner, whoever can stand the pain will win. We are stronger because we have less to lose. The majority have nothing to lose."

After taxes his greatest aggravation was the Israeli

rationing of the water needed by the growers of Gaza, which he saw as yet another criminal tactic to strangle the economy and subjugate the people. Here was another Palestinian persuaded that the Jews were stealing water from Gazans. He was certain that inside the Green Line, dividing Israel from the territories, there were huge wells pumping water right out of the Strip.

But cuts in water were being made to Israeli farmers too, from thirteen to twenty-five percent that year. An editorial in *The Jerusalem Post,* recalling how the nation's first prime minister David Ben-Gurion encouraged research into conservation, treatment and desalination of water, making Israel a leader in this field, complained of the waste and mismanagement. "Since then development has been stifled, and water has ceased to be a top national concern," the editorial said. Cheap water for irrigation encouraged enormous waste and overpumping which caused the depletion of reserves and the contamination of aquifers with sewage, according to the editorial. It pointed out whenever the Treasury requested a needed rise in agricultural water rates, the Knesset Water Committee, made up of members of the farming community, refused, keeping the price of water artificially low. The situation was aggravated by a meager rainfall. The shortage was about a fifth of annual consumption. Prices were raised, not for farmers, but among urban consumers whose use only accounted for twenty percent.

Palestinians did not believe it, or much care. Victims did not worry about the men who were strangling them. "There is a shortage of water in Palestine," Mr. Shawa was saying. "The Israelis are taking our water for

the Jewish settlements here: I need a lot but not as much
as the citrus growers. Farmers are not allowed to grow
what they want, Israelis limit our crops. They don't
allow me, for example, to increase my citrus trees or
replace old and dying ones. No one can do this.

"Each small farm has a well and a pump. They
forced me to install a meter on my pump and every
month an employee from the Civil Administration
checks my pump. If I exceed the ration of water I am
fined and made to pay a high price. They are choking
us."

Other men swore to me that swimming pools in the
Jewish settlements in Gaza were filled and refilled with
the water denied the growers. Mr. Shawa was calm, and
low-keyed, compared to them, not a man given to wild
accusations. He was even cautious in his accusations.

"There are certain times when we believe our tele-
phones are tapped," he said and did not understand the
humor in that remark. It was a certainty at Marna House
and most of the Gaza lawyers had a tap too.

Few Gazans were free of a sense of persecution and
all knew their lives to be deformed. The intifada brought
them a confirmation of the destruction wrought on
them, they were clearer now about the damage done,
and why it could not be tolerated.

Even the fishermen were restricted and could not
take their boats out as far in the sea as they once had,
coming back with such good catches of tuna, sardines,
cod, shrimp, bass and other fish whose names Westerners did not know. Twelve men usually rented a launch,
working in teams of four in different shifts.

"We can only go out fifteen kilometers and we cannot achieve anything," said a fisherman named Khader. "Israeli law limits us since 1978, the year of Camp David. We appealed to the High Court of Israel because we were furious, we kept saying to the Israelis: This area is too small for all the Palestinian fishermen. There are five thousand of us. I am sorry to say we did not succeed, or come away with anything." The best months were April and May, the worst were June, July and August because the sea was heated and the fish were too far out, he said. No, he saw no industrial waste, the sea had not changed.

"We used to go to Egyptian water to get a lot of kinds of fish but they say for security reasons we cannot and I do not believe this and we cannot say this to them."

It cost two hundred shekels for each man to pay for his share of the boat rental, gas and ice were another one hundred shekels over a three-day period. This meant an outlay equivalent to one hundred and fifty dollars. His earnings used to be adequate to easily cover expenses. Now he was lucky to take home fifteen dollars a day.

The I.D.F. patrolled the sea in their own launches and sometimes punished fishermen by filling their rented boats with water. The Gazans always sold their catches to the vendors on the waterfront who ran a fish market and charged them five percent commission. The fisherman had been out before dawn that day and came home with some mangoes and enough fresh shrimp on ice for his wife and six children. His wife gave us slices of the fruit. He wanted to sleep, he wanted to say that

Gazans knew how to wait for their independent state. "After two years or ten years that's okay," he said. "But it must come. We have to have this."

There were days when men and their families would sit on the beach to watch the sun set and fool a foreigner into thinking Gaza was a now strangely serene place. The Palestinians were accustomed to being watched or filmed or questioned by outsiders but each month fewer journalists came back, only returning in a swarm in August when I.D.F. decided to show them the procedures for Palestinians getting the new magnetic ID cards. General Arye Shifman, head of the Civil Administration, addressed the press and took questions. The ABC correspondent compared the new cards to those needed by blacks in South Africa. Such a remark hardly pleased the small plump general who had a sharp French face but he expected the day to be of benefit. The Palestinians were the animals in the zoo. The ID cards were only another use of high technology to keep the population submissive. It gave the Civil Administration even greater control over Gazan men, who could not work in Israel without the new cards. A security check was done on every man who applied but even those who had prison records and were suspected of political subversion often got the cards the first time. But in six months, or less, cards had to be renewed and then the Israelis were quick to deny them. The Gazans were warned that if they refused to go to their jobs in Israel residents of the West Bank might take their place.

It did not occur to the Israelis that it was not a pretty montage for the foreign press to see: hundreds of Gazan men on line for the precious card, squatting in line, or squeezed together in a tent down the line. No man dared speak as the soldiers hovered, only a few managed not to look fearful or sad. An I.D.F. officer was deeply offended to hear criticism. He thought the day was going very well, an efficient operation.

The worst of it was watching the Palestinians sit for a few seconds in a small room where a computer took their photograph. Every one of them looked as though he were going to the gallows but each man sat very straight, chin raised.

It was a slow summer and no one bothered to follow the United States Ambassador to Israel, William Brown, when he paid a quick visit to Gaza. He stopped at Marna House, which was the only place where his car could be safely and easily parked and the advance Shin Bet combed the grounds as if there might be a weapons cache in the larkspur, explosives in the shrubbery. Alya bestowed her most ghostly smile on the men and took her revenge: "It's quite safe," she said. "We have our own security here." It was harder for Malika to see the hated men poking, peering and roaming her property, even the little garden where the tomatoes and cucumbers grew. Her little face grew bright and mischievous for days afterward when she would remark how unwashed the Shin Bet men looked, really it was amazing that they were not obliged to be just a bit cleaner.

In August one hundred and twelve children were shot with live rounds, two boys in the one to five age group, fifteen in the six to ten group plus two girls, and ninety boys between the ages of eleven to fifteen and three girls as well. Many of the correspondents based in Jerusalem and Tel Aviv had been sent off to cover his-

toric breaking stories: China in June, then Eastern
Europe. Many of them said the intifada was withering,
kaput, the story over. After dinner in Marna House the
delegations sat in the large living room watching films
on the VCR. Copies of documentaries had been sent to
Alya in gratitude for her hospitality and endless patience
by producers in different countries. It was not illegal
since the films had all been cleared by the Israeli censor
and already aired. No one had better archives than Alya.

While the intifada went on in the dark the foreigners who could not see the struggle for themselves
watched it on the big set, an irony not lost on everyone.
They could watch Bob Simon of CBS, the exceptionally
astute correspondent covering Israel and the Occupied
Territories, doing his report on a December day at Ahli
Arab Hospital when there was no news from Gaza, only
a stream of injured teenagers being carried into the
emergency room. It was a year after the intifada began.
"Some days when I come to work it looks like a pediat-
rics ward," said an American, Dr. Leila Richards in his
broadcast.

For the first few months of the intifada television
and print coverage had been enormous and the stories
often shocking. In February 1988 there were two most
disturbing reports. The press filed an account of how
Israeli soldiers tried to bury alive four young Palestinians
who had been throwing stones. The army driver of a
bulldozer nearby was ordered to run over the beaten
men, refused, but then was willing to cover the uncon-
scious Arabs with dirt. Not until the army left the West
Bank village of Salim was it safe for the villagers to begin
digging and lifting out the bodies.

Many who heard about the incident could not believe it. In his own story for *The New York Times* which ran February 16, 1988, John Kifner explained that "it is being widely reported only now because many of the Israeli and foreign correspondents crisscrossing the West Bank had assumed it was too outlandish to be more than a rumor." General Amram Mitzna defended the conduct of the troops on the West Bank under his command by describing this behavior as "exceptional."

At a news conference he spoke like a civilized man, bestowing the words that so many needed to hear. The general said: "We, the Israelis, the Jews, have a very sensitive conscience." It was a contradiction, of course, of the declaration made only a few weeks earlier by the Defense Minister Yitzhak Rabin, who announced a policy of "force, might, beatings."

Eight days after the story broke on the attempt to suffocate living men Bob Simon did the most famous and startling broadcast of the intifada and a clip of his film was often seen in documentaries on the uprising. It showed four Israeli soldiers kicking two Palestinians on the ground, then one man bringing rocks down on a prisoner to break his collarbone and arm. It happened in the West Bank town of Nablus, almost at the hour that George Schultz, Secretary of State in the Reagan administration, was arriving in Israel for a futile final push to start negotiations to end the conflict.

The film of the soldiers, their feet and faces, the prisoners curling on the ground, was horrifying but the language that went with it was searing. Simon was the last of a generation of gifted foreign correspondents at CBS, not given to the leaden phrase, the trite and shallow wrap-up. Americans who thought of most television reporters as nitwits were often surprised by Simon's foreign broadcasts. The educated man used wit and irony very nicely in his stories and his deep calm on the air sometimes shaped itself into a form of faint mournfulness. He had been covering Israel off and on since 1977 and was very much at home living and working in that country. More than most Simon read an immense number of books, loved his own language and knew how to exercise its fine power. As a Fulbright scholar in France he studied French nineteenth-century intellectual history although, he always liked to say, much time was spent skiing or courting Francoise Arnaud, whom he married. He taught American literature in Lyon the second year of his scholarship.

In the broadcast seen in the United States on the "CBS Evening News," February 25, 1988, Simon did not placate or excuse. He seemed to be speaking without notes, a stand-up as it is called.

"Much is done in the Middle East in what passes for the heat of passion. This seemed cold, deliberate, methodical. . . . Israel's chief of staff said yesterday, force should never be used once someone has been captured or as a means of punishment. Hospitals in the West Bank and Gaza are full of young Arabs with broken arms. This is how it's done: multiple fractures with a rock. The boys did not scream. They did not beg . . ."

When Simon, with an English producer sent from London and a CBS cameraman, Moise Alpert, first saw those two Palestinians being chased up a steep and rugged hill, he wanted to follow. An accomplished skier and tennis player, Simon was sure he could catch up with the pursuers. But Moise Alpert, a man famous for his nature and wildlife documentaries, thought it impossible for middle-aged men to make that race and suggested that he film it instead from the distance where they stood. That day he had the special lens with him that he used so often to film birds and animals. So they watched as Alpert recorded the soldiers who thought what they were doing was a secret.

The last words of the broadcast were not timid: "American support over the last forty years has helped save the Israelis from their Arab enemies. George Schultz's mission may be to save the Israelis from themselves."

The correspondent was on vacation in France when the film aired and did not know at first the uproar it provoked. It was shown on Israeli television—along with a clip of the victims throwing stones before being caught as if to justify the reprisal—on other networks in the United States, in Europe, in Latin America and segments of it, without his words, in more than one report. Simon, a Jew who grew up in Great Neck, Long Island, was not himself reviled. But Moise Alpert, whose Lithuanian grandfather founded kibbutz Afikim in Galilee in 1931, received so many menacing messages and letters that CBS hired bodyguards for him, and more guards to watch their office in Tel Aviv. Simon even went on his own to the kibbutz to ask people about Alpert, whose company Afikim Productions was a major source of income for their collective. He needed to find out if people really wanted Moise harmed. They did not. One of the letters sent in hatred to Mr. Alpert was written on many folds of Israeli toilet paper. He was, in the eyes of those who wrote him, a debased and traitorous Jew, an Arab lover.

Some Israelis knew shame; one of them was a psychologist in Tel Aviv who said to *The New York Times* after the incident at Salim: "Israelis have a certain kind of ideal of the Israeli soldier, that he will handle himself with decency. These are the kinds of things other armies do—the French in Algeria, the Americans in Vietnam." In its annual report on human rights in countries around the world in 1988, the State Department report said Israeli troops had caused "many avoidable deaths and injuries" by firing on Palestinians. In a summation the report noted: "366 Palestinians were killed in 1988 as a result of the uprising," most of them by the Israeli Defense Forces, and "over 20,000 Palestinians were wounded or injured by the I.D.F." It also cited the demolition of the houses of one hundred and eight Arabs accused but "not convicted of involvement in security incidents." The Israeli deportation of thirty-six Palestinians was regarded by the United States as a violation of the Geneva Convention. The report also questioned the Israeli Army's assertion that its use of plastic bullets reduced the number of fatal injuries.

It made hardly any difference. Change did not come to Gaza. There were protests, denials, explanations from Israel's leaders who were displeased that their oldest, most benevolent ally would permit this. A *New York Times* reporter was sent to Tel Aviv to do a military analysis on the Israeli Army and the problems it faced putting down the Palestinians. "Israeli soldiers do not see themselves as cruel for the way they have put down the riots. They resent even the suggestion and are quick to blame journalists for the bad image the Army has suffered," he wrote.

Their traditional training was, he noted, not suited to the uprising.

There was concern in the United States that Israel's image was being damaged. But Eytan Gilboa, a political scientist at the Rothberg School for Overseas Students at the Hebrew University of Jerusalem, wrote in an article for *Orbis, A Journal of Public Affairs,* that the uprising was not hurting the loyalty that Americans traditionally felt for Israel.

The coverage in the United States was, in her opinion, highly critical of Israel. According to her study of the television reports on the "unrest," as she called it, aired on the ABC, CBS and NBC evening broadcasts between December 9, 1987 and April 4, 1988: "Israel was the target of twice as much negative, judgmental reporting as the protestors." Nine out of ten sources criticized Israel's treatment of Palestinians, she noted.

The three major U.S. television networks ran three hundred and seventy-five stories about the uprising, averaging three a day. *The New York Times* published two hundred and forty-two stories, an average of two a day and a total of four thousand two hundred and seventy-six column inches of text. *The Washington Post* also printed about two articles a day, one-fourth of them on the front page, totaling over three hundred thousand words.

"Did this barrage of critical commentary diminish the support that Americans traditionally gave Israel? Surprisingly, perhaps, it did not. And in that sense, we may say, the uprising failed to achieve one of its main purposes," Dr. Gilboa wrote in the first paragraph, then proceeded with data, tables, and analysis, proving herself right.

In Gaza they did not know this was one of their main purposes. Great strategists had not ordered the intifada and even Yasir Arafat did not know it was coming and was obliged to pay more attention to his constituency when it did.

In the first year of the intifada Marna House bulged with foreigners and sometimes, to amuse themselves, visitors in 1989 would read their names in the guest book which everyone always had to sign. Every day Alya had forms to send to the police on who was staying at the hotel. The register read like a temperature chart. In December 1987 an Italian photojournalist Sergio Ciglutti checked in but others only came for the day, rushing back to transmit their photographs. The great stampede had started: Italians, British, Americans, Swedes, Japanese, West Germans, Belgians, Austrians and Danes checked in at Marna House. The Spaniards and French followed. So did Jordanian engineers, a Swiss economist, a German electrician, United Nations personnel and a Dutch diplomat from Cairo. You were always obliged to give your profession in the guest book.

There was a torrent of journalists, writers on assignment, television producers and crews making documentaries. People slept three to a room and were happy to have any bed at all. The American humorist P. J. O'-Rourke, who described Gaza as "Hell's Riviera," came on the eighteenth of January, then sixteen Brazilian doctors and thirteen Brazilian nurses whom Alya always remembered with fondness. She favored those in the medical profession although recognizing that journalists, although so much more trouble, were also helpful. Five Italian doctors arrived in March, so did a make-up artist from Antwerp with three Belgian filmmakers. The delegations, on their fact-finding missions, were often an odd mix: a chiropractor from California, a priest and a restaurateur both from Missoula, Montana. And a British actor named Winston Springer was there in May.

"We were so busy I had to ask people to do their own bills, just to leave what they owed," said Alya.

The delegations did not stay long in the second year of the intifada for Gaza, a tiny enclave, could not compete with Jerusalem or the West Bank with its haunting landscape. Little Gaza—one-fifteenth the size of the West Bank—was a punitive place for foreigners so they rarely stayed more than a day or one night. "You cannot even see the sea," said one foreigner. All through 1989 groups kept coming in chartered buses or vans. They did their duty, touring the camps, talking to Palestinians who spoke English and would come to meet them at Marna House.

Hoping to learn, some of the visitors to Gaza that year learned far more than they expected and felt sudden shock or grief that was new and astonishing. In the spring a Canadian delegation sitting in a van, in Rafah, near the Egyptian border, saw a Palestinian woman walking down the road when she was shot. Perhaps the Israeli soldier was aiming at a rebellious boy but the bullet went to her. No one dared move fearing they too would be shot. That night the leader of the group assembled all of them in the living room with its long pea-colored couch, the deep old armchairs and the little upright ones with striped seats, the piano no one played, the fireplace rarely lit, so everyone could vent their feelings. It was a precaution so no one would buckle under from stress. On June fourth, twelve Americans from Quaker groups around the United States, all working on a Middle East Education Program, came to Gaza for one night during a three-week tour. But Gaza was placed under total curfew for ten days to ensure there were no disturbances marking the twenty-second anniversary of the Israeli annexation in the Six-Day War.

It was Sunday. They went to a briefing at the office of the public information office of the United Nations Relief and Works Agency, a routine call, and were then turned back at the Jabalia Camp by soldiers. The rest of the day, various people from the international relief organizations in Gaza came to the garden to brief them since it was impossible for the Quakers to easily circulate in town. Outside, the war grew noisy: rounds of ammunition, men yelling, the soft plop of tear gas grenades. Their duties were over when a Palestinian came racing up the driveway to tell Alya that someone had been shot and was dead. The corpse was in a backyard on the same block, a few houses down. The thirty-two-year-old head of the delegation wasn't sure at first whether the Americans were being asked to see the dead man. "Is this disrespectful?" he asked, not wishing to offend. No, no, the messenger said, the family and friends want you to see what has happened.

Alya, who considers all foreigners at Marna House to be under her care since so few speak any Arabic, thought it unwise to walk down the street when the soldiers were patrolling. So all of them, the Quakers and the Palestinian woman, used chairs to climb over the garden wall to reach the dead man without being sighted. He lay in a small hut, on the ground, in back of a house, under the very clean white sheet Muslims use for the dead. His face was uncovered so the Quakers could see for themselves that he had been shot twice in the head, once between the eyes. A lantern gave the only light but everyone stared at the small holes in his forehead. There was not much left of the back of his skull, the bullets had shattered bone, blood vessels and brain. The blood still made pools which wet peoples' shoes if they stood too close for the dead can keep bleeding. The best friend of the dead man, also in his early twenties, fainted at one point when he realized the corpse could not come back to life. More people came to the hut. The best friend said the other man had taunted an Israeli patrol as it passed them on the street and the marksman, after such a quick success, began the usual macabre celebration, clapping his hands or yelling with glee over his kill. The Americans did not choose to leave the hut. The parents and the grandmother came, behaving as everyone does in sudden sorrow.

It was learned that the dead man was the only son in a family of eight children and was to be married in a week.

"We stayed there with the people, we shared in their grief," one American said. "A doctor came and said he was shot by high velocity bullets. He thought he had been shot at fifty meters. Only a few of us spoke Arabic but words were not important."

There was some confusion about when the body could be buried, which Moslems do immediately. Many

Gazans refuse to let the Israeli authorities do autopsies believing that they will remove crucial organs for their own research, or even transplants, which they cannot permit. They bury their dead in secret. It was finally sorted out and the last victim of that day in June was carried away. The close friend needed to say a last thing to the foreigners' group, before they went out of their lives forever: "Go to America and tell people this is an intifada for peace." All the Quakers could do was to call upon their own quiet powers so they held a silent worship in the living room of Marna House, holding hands, some faces still wet. Alya had never seen anything like it.

The next day they departed and kept an appointment at the Jaffee Center for Strategic Studies, a military think tank at Tel Aviv University. The Quakers remained intact. The students at the university reminded them of the young Americans seen on every campus but so different from the Palestinians they had wanted to comfort only the night before. The Quakers later asked that their names and those of their groups not be disclosed for fear the Israelis would prevent their return.

It was only one death, of course, but months later the visitors, not disposed to dramatic revelations, could not forget any of it: the young face with the dark holes in the forehead, the close friend lying on the ground to be near the man he had loved, the lantern, how hands grasped other hands in a hut, the clasp of strangers who did not have a common tongue and came from such different civilizations. One man remembered what he had written in his notes, the last words after their final briefing in the garden: "This has been a quiet day in Gaza."

Some of the Americans asked Alya where they might leave a token of their sympathy, just a small gift of cash for the family of the shot man. Alya said no. She always said no. She did not want foreigners to think that the Palestinians had their hands out, or that giving money was a solution of any kind. She told the Americans it would be better if they went home and worked for peace.

"We want a clean name," she would say. "We are not beggars. Our name must be beautiful and clean."

Everyone knew that the P.L.O. provided for many families of the arrested or slain but sometimes the money did not come for months.

In Gaza the weather was wonderful in the spring and summer, exactly what a resort might boast of in a brochure. Even in August the heat, so much less brutal than in New York or Dallas, would lift by the end of each day. The silence every night, when the curfew began, was never soothing. It was as though all of Gaza was given over to a sudden sickness. After dinner the foreigners at Marna House, unable to go out in the stifled town, and unwilling to go to their rooms to read or write up their notes, would drift into the garden, preferring the chairs below the branches of the healthy ficus tree.

There were a few Europeans from nongovernmental agencies—the NGO's, they are called—who would take coffee outside and talk to each other in the kind night air about their budgets or aid projects in the Occupied Territories. Sometimes something hidden would show through in the conversation, sending up a strange glint.

An Englishwoman had a small story to tell and spoke in a low voice so the men at the table had to bend slightly to hear. She was not operatic or even indignant just rueful. It was only an account of a humiliating and unnecessary delay at a checkpoint, the insolent soldier enjoying himself. She knew the territories well and how to handle the Israelis but this time had been deeply upset. There were a hundred versions of the story, such encounters were common. Perhaps it was how the soldiers entertained themselves.

"And I thought to myself 'You bloody Jew,'" the woman said. "Then I was so horrified that I had to ring up my best friend—she is a Jew—in England to tell her." The friend had been consoling and told the woman, really, not to worry.

The Europeans said nothing but the little story jarred. One man looked up at the moon and another arranged the coffee cups on a tray to take inside. The night watchman, who had said his last prayer at eight P.M., was dozing. Alya preferred her guests to go upstairs before eleven P.M. but did not say anything unless she knew them well. Breakfast was at seven.

II

Punishment and Love

On the fateful day, december 9, 1987, the lawyer Raji Sourani left home early in Gaza to drive to Jerusalem to join a group of other Palestinians and Israelis opposed to the occupation in the territories. "We wanted to explain and protest and warn," said Mr. Sourani later. None of them knew this would be a historic date, that the moment was at hand.

He went with two other prominent Gazans, both physicians, Dr. Zakari Aga and Dr. Haidar Abdel Shafi, who also spoke. The Israelis, equally passionate about Palestinian self-determination, were a professor of chemistry, Israel Shahak, a survivor of the Bergen-Belsen concentration camp and head of the Israeli League for Human and Civil Rights, his friend the history teacher Dr. Joseph Algazy and the famous lawyer Felicia Langer who for years had been defending Palestinians in the Israeli courts.

The press conference at eleven a.m. in Beit Agron, the government press office, was well-attended but that afternoon a Palestinian journalist brought the news that an explosion had taken place in Gaza. The word "intifada" does not mean uprising in Arabic but rather "shaking off" yet this became the word that everyone used.

Nothing was to be the same after the struggle started. To the Israelis who ran Gaza and the Strip the thirty-five-year-old attorney had long been a thorn in their throat. As the resistance spread and hardened, as the unity of the Palestinians threatened Israel's supremacy, men like Raji Sourani could hardly be tolerated. In five years he was arrested and incarcerated four times but that only made him a more powerful presence for the best men were put in prison and it was expected of male patriots.

No one in the region was more admired or needed than this intense, intelligent defense lawyer with his open, ardent allegiance to the P.L.O. and the constant challenge he raised in the military courts, which judged all Palestinians suspected of subversion. Over and over he made clear the abuses of the occupation so foreigners labeled him a human rights lawyer or advocate and the abuses went on. He was under surveillance.

Yet Raji Sourani did not act in a secretive manner, not a man to speak in whispers, always mindful of the tapped telephone, the bugged room, the ingratiating informer.

"I don't hide too much," Mr. Sourani said. "What I say in my home and my office I say to anyone."

His wife and his mother worried about Raji's nerves, the frequency of Raji's headaches, a recurrence of the duodenal ulcer which required surgery when he was only twenty, the strain that stamped his face and changed his speech. It was dangerous, grinding, disturbing work which was eating his life in huge bites. It had led to torture and imprisonment but this was a man who long ago took a vow and had never wavered.

The lawyer could often do very little and was not informed in many cases of the charges against a client. "It's like confronting a ghost," he said. On Omar Mukhtar Street his office had only four rooms for four lawyers so one man had to work in a small waiting room which needed more chairs. People stood to wait their turn. There were no computers and only one telephone line for a second was impossible to obtain.

The poor kept coming. Or he went to them, to the courts and to the prisons, no day long enough to see them all, driving so fast that his license was taken away for three years. No one who ever knew him could say that he was a prudent driver. By taking away his license for so long the Israelis had kept him alive—he admitted as much and swore he had learned his lesson. Sometimes the ordinary harassments made him wild. Remembering his frustration at being stopped at checkpoints more than ten times when he had to leave Gaza to see prisoners—the largest number were in Ansar III, a two-and-a-half-hour drive—or to appear in court, Mr. Sourani imitated himself questioning the military: "Why did you take my ID card away? Why am I standing here? Why doesn't someone tell me when my ID card will be given back?" They kept him suspended.

There was never a pretense on his part at being neutral, or outside the P.L.O., although his own family were not refugees but from an old aristocratic clan of educated merchants and landowners with property and orchards and a name no less mighty than the Shawas. The orchards had not been taken away since their site was not suitable for a Jewish settlement so his own family had been spared. Nevertheless he was always thinking of the old Palestine, of the cities that had been theirs.

"No one can forget or abandon the idea that Lod and Jaffa belong to Palestine," Mr. Sourani said.

It was the old lament, a lifelong habit, although men knew that Lod and Jaffa were gone forever. They did not live in a daze.

"Look, politics is not controlled by emotions. If

there are negotiations with the Palestine National
Council and the Executive Committee of the P.L.O.
then we will accept their decisions," said Mr. Sourani.
"These are the legal bodies."

The truthful man was first arrested in September
1979 for being a member of the Popular Front for the
Liberation of Palestine, which he admits. Sentenced by
a military court to three years he was sent to Gaza
Central jail, a place he came to know so well. He had
only been out of law school two years and was training
in the office of an older, distinguished lawyer in Gaza
named Fraj Saraf, a Christian and a nationalist but not
of a specific faction.

By the summer of 1985 his own office to provide
legal aid had been open for two years and he knew now
the cases of many men who during interrogation had
often wished to die, and come close enough. He had six
cases of beatings until death, he had dossiers on men
with injuries that sometimes even shocked him. There
was an engineer, thirty-three, from Rafah who told the
lawyer there was something wrong with his head. Mr.
Sourani was visiting the man in Gaza jail. He repeated
what the prisoner told him: "During the interrogations
they beat me with a ruler on the center of my skull. I
began to feel such pain, and terrible headaches, so I
could hardly bear it. The skin on the skull came off."
There were no mirrors, the prisoner felt this with his
fingers. Mr. Sourani was startled but slightly skeptical so
the man took off the bandage on his head wanting the
lawyer to see for himself. It was true.

"I saw the bone of the skull in this—hole," Mr.
Sourani said. "There was inflammation and he was rub-

bing the marks on his head." The round, youthful face of the lawyer, always so alive, was sketched in sorrow when he described the ordeal of this man, or that man, an endless line of them. Often he was not permitted to see his clients until they were brought into court wearing the blue overalls of the prisoner, shuffling, dazed, with yellowish or swollen faces. Sometimes men found it hard to speak. The Shin Bet did not care if the man showed how he had been assaulted and it did not appear to disturb the judge.

"I was visiting my clients in the jail, fifty or sixty clients," said Mr. Sourani. "The Israelis thought that I had raised too many complaints and I was rude." He was standing by the interior gate on a Sunday that July in 1985 when an Israeli, grinning, approached him and said there was an "invitation" for Raji Sourani who was expected inside. There was nothing he could do to prepare himself. It went very fast: he had to change into the blue overalls and be handcuffed and hooded. There were seven or eight Shin Bet men waiting for him who were very pleased, almost gleeful to see him. He could not see but he could count the different voices.

" 'At last we have Raji!' they kept saying," Mr. Sourani said. "As if they had arrested someone who has thrown a hundred grenades." His real name was Raja but no one ever called him that.

Then the usual: taunts and ridicule when he claimed the right to inform his office or his family, the hood kept over his head, the lack of sleep for five nights. But the ceaseless interrogations lasted for forty-three consecutive days, sometimes only for one hour a day and then five or six sessions a day and at night. He remembered all of it: the command to remain standing, the three days without food, the guard who had to escort him to the toilet, and the things he told himself to keep from going under. During the worst of it he heard himself making peculiar uncontrollable noises and there was the brief lovely delusion that he was in a hospital with his much loved six-year-old nephew, both of them safe. He confessed to nothing, repeating over and over to himself that if he could not defend his own person then he was not worthy of being a lawyer for all the other Palestinians.

All the prisoners hated the hooding and found that after only a few hours it could provoke startling episodes of madness. The man not allowed to sleep, barely able to breathe inside the hood smelling of old sweat and old vomit, may suffer a temporary spell of insanity and this sensory deprivation, as the doctors called it, was often as terrible to bear as the beatings. The Israelis found it a useful method to induce acute disorientation, so had the British in Northern Ireland. It was an easy way to inflict deep harm.

"I know myself better than you do, I did not do anything outside the law," Mr. Sourani kept saying to the interrogators. It was true, he had chosen to be a lawyer not a combatant but too many people looked up to him, which made him dangerous. The Shin Bet agents were Israelis who spoke Arabic very well although he was fluent in Hebrew, and in English too. It was in his own language that he was being mocked and threatened.

"One of the worst times I ever faced was when I began to lose all sensation. I decided I must sit down and they began to beat me so I reacted in an unwilling way, kicking out at them. An officer said 'What's wrong Raji?' I managed to say that I felt very bad and had to have some rest."

They took the hood off for the beatings so he saw this Shin Bet officer sitting with his feet up on a desk, the picture of a man completely relaxed, and confident.

"Crucify him," the Israeli said to others. It was the order to shackle the prisoner on an iron door with bars, one arm manacled high above his head and the other arm below his waist so the body could not be straightened. And this is how he stayed until he fainted and found himself back in his cell.

In the beginning he had tried to answer back, to argue and reason. On the fifth day of the questioning before dawn—someone told him it was ten to three in the morning—a Shin Bet gave him advice: "You tell your story and we leave you alone." He remembered what he tried to say: "I am not a kid who builds a house in the sand and then rubs it out with his foot." There was no story to tell that they wanted to hear and he kept saying so, always a luxury the prisoner cannot afford. He was slow to accept that.

"You bloody Nazi, this is barbarous," Mr. Sourani recalled saying to one Shin Bet officer. He was whipped with a sandal and the guard was told to keep the prisoner on his feet, to not allow him to rest for a second. Sometimes he would start crying. Wanting to honor all the men who had gone before him in that grimy, desolate room Mr. Sourani only learned what the poorest of men had once found out. It was only to be borne if you thought of all of those who had gone before you, the others who had crawled through every inch and every minute of it.

"I was lucky to pass through this experience, many hundreds and hundreds of men have been through much worse," he said.

Sometimes he could talk about it quite calmly, wanting to speak in a detached way as a lawyer might.

"Beatings from my experience are the simplest thing to do," Mr. Sourani said. "They are very proficient. And when they put this hood on your head, saturate it with water and close it—well, if it is closed for forty seconds you are deeply thinking you are going to die. They expel tear gas inside it too." In 1985 he was moved from jails in Gaza, to Beersheba, back to Gaza and then to Ashkelon. He petitioned the court that to be jailed in Israel was a violation of the Geneva Convention of August 1949 but did not succeed.

So many people have climbed the stairs to his apartment in the building which the Souranis own: his mother and an aunt live on the ground floor, his brother, a dentist, and his wife above them, and on the top floor, Raji and his wife, Amal, who was ten years younger than her husband and studied at a university on the West Bank to be an economist. She remembered that they were watching television at seven-thirty in the evening on March 23, 1988, when the bell rang. Soldiers were outside and took him promptly without a rampage. The mother, seeing the jeeps and trucks, rushed out wanting to kiss her son as he was being led off. Amal Sourani stayed silent and did not speak or weep. She only looked at her husband not the men crowding around him. There were only seven but she saw a sea of them.

"There were many, many," Mrs. Sourani said. "I was very nervous but I pretend not to be."

So many people have sat for hours in their living room on the little white couch, in the comfortable white chairs around the table with the china figurine, a wedding present. The nice furniture was made in Gaza. Raji was often too drained or distracted to see foreigners but thought if he turned them away it would be a sign of submission. It was Amal Sourani who always opened the door and did not appear to resent the visitors although they devoured his time when so little was left for her. The happy marriage, in its third year, knew unusual strains.

There had been an earlier arrest in December 1986, the year of his wedding, in the "little intifada" as Gazans called it, a year before the mass uprising. He was only held for twenty days.

In 1988, there was no interrogation and no charges for he was an administrative detainee, who could be held for six months, the usual period of time until the following summer when the detention was extended to a year. He was shuttled from Ansar II in Gaza to Ansar III in Israel, then back to Ansar II and finally returned to Gaza jail to serve the rest of the sentence. Transferring inmates was seen by the authorities as a way of avoiding the creation of a strong leadership inside the prisons. The arrest was seen as retaliation for his role in the Gazan lawyers' strike that lasted from December 1987 to October 1988, when they refused to continue being involved in "sham justice," his words.

"I kept saying, 'We can't be used as a legal cover for organized crime,' " Mr. Sourani said. Attempting to justify the lawyers' strike to a judge in a Gaza military court in January 1988 he was held in contempt and warned not to speak in "political terms." There were three hundred and twenty lawyers in Gaza but while support of the strike was total only a small fraction of them defended those suspected of subversion or the various security offenses. It always put them at risk or perhaps they saw it as futile. Raji Sourani was such an irritant in the military courts that he was even barred from them for the entire year in 1986. It was always his habit to send records of his most egregious cases to the organization in Ramallah called Al Haq/Law in the Service of Man, the West Bank affiliate of the International Commission of Jurists which was formed by Palestinians in 1979.

He had never been a prisoner in Ansar III until that spring in 1988. The Israelis called it Ketziot detention camp but the Palestinians named both Ansar II and Ansar III after the "Ansar" built for prisoners of war during the Israeli invasion of Lebanon in 1982. Ansar means "supporters" in Arabic and was used for the followers of the prophet Mohammed when he escaped from Mecca, a hostile city, to Medina where he ruled his rapidly growing empire. "Imprisonment is only one way of preventing violence in the territories," said Colonel David Tsemack, the prison commander, to an Israeli reporter. Others were certain that it was one reason for the uprising.

The colonel, the man who built the first Ansar in Lebanon, was one of the officials who shot dead two prisoners during a riot but the case was investigated and no charges were brought against him.

Some forty miles south of Beersheba, in the heart of the Negev desert, Ansar III was a vast world of tents, paved roads and barbed wire, three perimeters of it fencing each section of prisoners. It was the largest prison for the Palestinians. Families never came to visit, only the lawyers and occasional delegations of civil rights groups, and those few foreign journalists of sufficient importance whose ties to Israel were above question. In winter, the cold was biting and in the summer temperatures rose to one hundred degrees, higher inside the tents. There were twenty-five to twenty-eight men in a tent which was sixteen by thirty-two feet. Some men were administrative detainees and a larger number that summer were those awaiting trial or already convicted. The attorneys were allowed to bring a few clothes and personal possessions but packages could not be mailed.

Such stringent, unreasonable conditions were imposed for any families wishing to see prisoners that visits were impossible.

Some eminent Americans sought out Raji Sourani on their fact-finding trips. When Judge Marvin Frankel, an attorney and former professor of law at Columbia University, was allowed to see Mr. Sourani the prisoner showed him how not all of the five spigots at a water trough worked. One hundred and thirty-five men used them for washing and drinking. There were no showers, only wooden rooms where naked prisoners could wash if they carried in water. Buckets were not provided so the men used their cups. The prisoner described the food, which was inadequate and insufficient, and how no one was allowed to leave the tent at night to go to the latrine.

In so many ways Raji Sourani remained his old valiant self.

On a second fact-finding trip, another member of the Lawyer's Committee, the Executive Director Michael Posner, interviewed the Palestinian on August 17, 1988. He was told by Raji Sourani that on his transfer from Ansar III to Ansar II he was blindfolded and hit and beaten every half hour. He thought rifle butts and clubs were used. When he complained, a lit cigarette was pressed into his hand by a soldier and the lawyer shouted in Hebrew: "If you are an officer and a man you can shoot me, but if you do this to me, you are a coward!" He remembered the soldier saying: "We are not going to kill you—we will do it in a different way!"

What Judge Frankel and Mr. Posner reported was published in a Lawyer's Committee report in 1988, *An Examination of Detention of Human Rights Workers and Lawyers from the West Bank and Gaza and Conditions of Detention at Ketziot.*

There is one fleeting episode, a brief conversation, not mentioned in any report but which Mr. Sourani has always remembered. The man whose mind was taken over by hate, the fanatic, would not have revealed it.

After spending five days in Ansar II the prisoner was being taken to Gaza jail in a military van when an Israeli officer, guessing he was an educated man, began speaking to him. "Are you a lawyer?" the officer asked for there were so many of them in the jails. When the prisoner held out his hands to be handcuffed it was the officer who said: "No need for that."

"Is it very bad?" asked the Israeli. The prisoner, in

a shaken state, answered abruptly: "Have you ever known anyone who was happy in jail?"

Because the officer was going back in the same van to Gaza jail he ordered a soldier sitting in the front seat to sit beside Mr. Sourani. When the prisoner started changing his seat in the van the soldier kicked him and he fell on the floor. The officer saw it and ordered the soldier to apologize. "What? To a terrorist?" the soldier asked and did not.

The lawyer was slow to appreciate the interference on his behalf from the kindly officer, knew that he had spoken rudely and apologized. "In the last month I have been treated as an animal but I thank you and I am deeply touched," said Mr. Sourani.

It was a short trip to the fortified compound of Gaza jail where the two men said goodbye.

"Then the gentle officer said to me: 'We will someday sit together and live in peace.' We shook hands and his eyes said everything." He always called this Israeli the "gentle officer."

He wanted to tell the little story so it might be known there were many such Jews and he never forgot this. Two of his closest friends were Israeli lawyers, Leah Tsemel and Tamar Peleg, who was on the staff of the Association for Civil Rights in Israel. Since the intifada both their names were well known in the Occupied Territories. When one of the women fell sick, or reached complete exhaustion, he worried about them as if they were a little family of their own. He saw Tamar Peleg more frequently and spoke, with wonder, of her calm and her strengths.

He always came home late but just once a visitor

found him sitting at home, in the afternoon, by himself
in the living room, watching an old American movie on
television. He said that television sometimes helped to
"freeze" his mind and stopped him from thinking. That
day a client, a thirteen-year-old boy, was sentenced to
three years for throwing stones.

"He was so small, at first I thought he was eleven,"
said Mr. Sourani. "His mother . . ." He turned off the
television and let the sentence dangle. It did not need
to be completed.

The parents of children under twelve who were
caught throwing stones were fined amounts ranging
from four hundred to fifteen hundred dollars because
they could not be sent to prison. To free children under
fourteen who were arrested for hurling stones meant the
parents had to pay bail which the I.D.F. raised from
seven hundred and fifty dollars to two thousand five
hundred. The sum was so huge that many parents could
not pay and the child twelve or over went to prison.

He was the historian of too much misery and knew
it and yet held to a happier opinion of human nature
than others could manage. It was better for him when
he was with company, the gregarious man needed
friends, needed to laugh and be distracted. In another
life he might have been a novelist and admired no one
more than the late Ghassan Kanafani, the Palestinian
writer who was assassinated by the Israelis in Beirut. The
militant exiled novelist was married to a Danish woman,
Annie, whom Mr. Sourani said was very wonderful in-
deed.

"Mossad put a bomb in the car and he was in it with
his most beloved person, a thirteen-year-old niece," said

Mr. Sourani, referring to the Israeli foreign intelligence agency. "He was a fighter, a journalist, a most intelligent, wonderful writer. I loved him very much, I was so affected by his writing. You could love him without knowing him."

He would mention Kanafani's books, *The Weapons, The Land of Sad Oranges* or *Men in the Sun,* as if they had been written by a brother, a man made of the same clay, the same skin. The writer always held to the old bitter theme of Palestinian survival, both territorial and political, and the indifference of the world to the lostness of the exiles. And every day the lawyer passed the face of Kanafani for in one corner of the living room was a portrait of him, a painting given by a friend, a cherished but illegal possession.

Such a different life was expected for Raji Sourani when he was growing up and knew only love and comfort and pleasure with the world. His mother doted and he pleased people without effort. There were eight children whose parents owned a farm and vast orchards. They were an old family with a proud history for their father's father, Mousa Sourani, had been arrested in Gaza in 1936 as the great rebellion began and held in administrative detention by the British. He belonged to the national movement led by the Mufti of Jerusalem, Haj Amin Husseini, and in 1949 was among the Palestinian leaders who established an All-Palestine Government in Gaza to regain Palestine within the mandatory boundaries. It failed. Raji Sourani said the men first met in their old family house, which was now abandoned and empty.

He was fourteen years old when the Israelis took

Gaza, met resistance and kept destroying it. But from that first day on he belonged to the P.L.O. as Mr. Sourani told the English journalist David Smith. The boy was borne along on the little waves of death each week and always tried to stay with the corpses of the martyrs until they were taken to the cemeteries as if by being a steadfast escort he was showing the great love due them. He took flowers to the families of the slain men and expected the patriots to be honored by all. But in the mosque dominated by the Muslim Brotherhood, the Islamic fundamentalists, his teacher was stern and reproachful, telling him: "We should not speak of politics" or "You must not cause trouble." It infuriated him so the perturbed and grieving boy, once so devout and obedient, left. The mosque, the brotherhood, the daily prayers, the saturating years of study and worship were forsaken.

Educated in Bethlehem at the Evangelical Lutheran School, where he studied English and German, he was required to attend chapel but always prayed as a Moslem on his own little rug that he had carried from home. But that child vanished forever when the occupation began. After Bethlehem there was a year in London which transformed him. He lived with the family of a pharmacist named Graves in Ealing Common, was much favored by the motherly wife, and explored the huge city as if his life depended on it.

"It was one of the richest periods of my life. In a way I began to learn to think. I went everywhere— museums, libraries, small neighborhoods. Someone said to me that a person living in London for twenty years couldn't know it better than I did."

Enrolled at the University of Beirut he often went to the larger, more famous campus of the American University of Beirut, founded in 1866, whose grounds looked like a lovely park. For young Palestinians in a delirium to take back their country, it was a paradise, blazing with speeches, vows, appeals, recruiters, for the young who were longing for a desperate glory.

"Beirut was very rich in education and I was so greedy. I was, in a very unique way, touched by George Habash. He came to Beirut in March 1973 and there was a sort of ceremony, unbelievably stormy, with not less than fifteen thousand people. He spoke. Believe me, when he was speaking, he was able to translate your pulse into words. The power, the optimism, was remarkable." Years later he would still insist that George Habash was the conscience of the Palestinian revolution and that his being Christian might have adversely affected the huge faction that he led, the Popular Front for the Liberation of Palestine. Mr. Sourani remembered that Dr. Habash had said, if only once: "I will forever blame God for making me a Christian." At the University of Alexandria in Egypt, where he studied law, Raji Sourani became a member of the P.F.L.P.

One of his own brothers was arrested in 1968 for belonging to the first cell of Fatah. But he chose another path, defending the poor. It was widely believed, and sometimes written by foreigners, that the P.L.O. financed Mr. Sourani's office but this was not the case although it paid for others.

"I don't receive a penny. I never asked," he said. "It is a matter of pride. And it's legally problematic." The funds came from the land although the income from the

citrus crops was sharply diminished as the Israelis prevented Palestinians from exporting their oranges and
lemons since this would prove competitive with their
own produce.

As the year ended he was still racing to keep up,
sometimes getting to the office shortly after seven-thirty
A.M. where people were already waiting. On a winter
morning there was a man sitting there with a mournful
aching face who looked ready to weep. When he was
notified by the army that his house was to be demolished
his last and only hope was for an injunction to forestall
it.

"Twenty-three orders for the demolition of houses
in the last fifty days," said Mr. Sourani in the last week
of December. People were not permitted to rebuild once
their houses were destroyed and did not have enough
money to build elsewhere. The necessary permits were
impossible to obtain. There was only the Red Cross who
gave out tents to the homeless families. Nothing upset
the Palestinians as deeply as the loss of their homes
except for murder.

The birthday of Raji Sourani was December 31 and
he was now thirty-six. On that day the family gathered
to mark the occasion with a quiet little party among
themselves. In Gaza the family holds the world together
and inside a circle of women who loved him Mr. Sourani
often smiled but could never imitate the happy boy he
once was. The next afternoon, New Year's Day, all of
them were sitting outside in the yard of their building.
The trees and shrubs and uncut grass made it a cheerful
haven behind the high walls that kept so many places
private. There was his mother, his aunt, the younger

brother with his wife and Amal, chatting and eating
outside, pleased with the day. The lawyer jumped to his
feet when I arrived, offered some dried candy and
showed me the squat tree in the yard whose fat leaves
were dried to make the sweet. *Molou'chia,* he wrote in
the notebook, the Arabic name of the candy. The mood
shifted slightly because I was there although it was only
to say goodbye. The questions were finally finished, the
notebooks filled, only the problem of how to avoid the
Israeli censor remained. But Mr. Sourani was reminded
again of his work and all the punishments, including his
own, that he had begun describing to me so many
months before. There was always a new tragedy and the
driven man began speaking of the thirteen-year-old girl
from Beit Hanoun, a village to the north, who had been
shot in the face at close range. Her right eye took a
rubber bullet, which is always believed to be so harmless.
In the Eye Hospital the Palestinian surgeon feared
shock and did not immediately tell her the eye had been
removed. But she knew all along that the socket was
empty beneath the thick bandage and did not once
shriek or rage. It happened in a schoolyard: the soldiers
were close and the pupils sent up a hail of stones. One
man sighted her and fired. It was thought that he aimed
at her face.

In the Eye Hospital, she was able to smile, a slight,
tremulous girl with the beginning of real beauty in the
small face. She was pleased to be given a bag of chocolates, which she hid under the sheet so that when finally
alone she could enjoy the treat. There were relatives and
friends ringing her bed. In Beit Hanoun members of the
large clan said that she was taking it very well and that

she had always been an unusual girl, not easily cowed, and smart. But some understood that she had not seen the wound where the eye had been and that the bandage could not stay on forever.

The lawyer did not know that I had already seen Eman Abdellaziz Zawaideh in the hospital and understood how courageous she would now always have to be.

"She was known for her beautiful eyes," said Mr. Sourani, the sadness thrust on his face again. He was taking her case.

The helmets of the soldiers could be seen above the walls in a familiar frieze but the lawyer pretended not to notice and the women would not turn their heads to look. It was the twenty-fifth anniversary of the founding of Fatah so the army was sweeping the streets, even the neighborhoods like Rimal with their villas and verandas and candy-trees, in case there was any sign of celebration or defiance.

Everyone sat still, upright as though a photograph was being taken that did not require them to smile. I thought that the soldiers might be coming for Raji for they had only to push open the gate. But he knew better. The soldiers always drove, then rushed to the door of the wanted man, they did not slowly circle in the streets. Even Amal knew as much.

The wrecked face of the girl, Eman, again hung over us and his final words were why he had agreed to take the case, which seemed a hopeless business. "To show the responsibility of the army toward the people and their unlawful practices," Mr. Sourani said. That was the trouble with him, he was still pushed by a stubborn steadfast faith that in the Israeli military courts he could hold an army of occupation to account and prove what they were doing was wrong. A friend of Raji Sourani thought that he did it out of love and would manage to last many more years. The answer seemed too vague. I expected to hear the word "honor"—*karameh* in Arabic—not love. Principles, not love, made more sense.

"Love—for the people, for Palestine, for the P.L.O.?" I asked, wanting specifics. "His grandfather?"

"Yes" was the answer. "Everything."

There was something else: it was always the lawyers like Raji Sourani who gave the families a measure of hope and who steadied them although their efforts were usually ineffectual. What people wanted most of all was to see the imprisoned men and were often denied these visits. Every week hundreds of them assembled on Beach Street near the sea to find out if permission was to be granted, an orderly and forlorn crowd keeping quite still as if attention must be paid even when nothing happened and no names were being called out. Tuesdays and Thursdays were for the men in Gaza jail, Fridays for Ansar II. Their silence seemed more tense and sad than any noise. People often carried thin plastic bags with presents, some underwear and socks since only clothing was permitted. It made many of the mothers frantic for in their minds they saw their sons, shrunken and waxy-faced, longing for home-cooked food. The army thought that messages could be smuggled inside the food but there were many other better ways to conceal a scrap of paper.

People stood or squatted or sat on scraps of paper under an old corrugated tin roof held up by poles, facing loops of old barbed wire to keep them apart from the soldiers across the road. Behind them was a wall and above the embankment two more soldiers watching all of us. There were no benches. The youngest males liked to stand on the wall as if they needed to look down on the soldiers facing them, not wishing to crouch and be made smaller. Their faces were locked, they learned how to do this for all their lives they had only heard commands: wait, stop, come here, go, get out. The wrong expression, too inflamed or hateful, could bring trouble.

No one read *Al-Quds*, the newspaper, and people did not chat. From time to time an Israeli soldier stepped forward and lifted a bullhorn. He read the Arabic names of a dozen prisoners who may have visitors that day. There were happy little grunts and exclamations if the names were those of a husband or son, and people surged forward to form a line, single file, so a soldier could check them. Then it began all over again for the others and a few women fidgeted and sighed or shifted their positions. Only one man was pacing, the others stood like sentries.

"He speaks so badly we don't even recognize the names," a woman complained, the dry, deeply creased face puckered and angry. This was the sixth week that she had come and she feared that her husband might be starving. It was harder for the women to understand the Israeli voice, only the men in Gaza went to Israel to work, were accustomed to Hebrew and even learned that language. They understood the names, that accent, well enough. Before the uprising, more than sixty thousand of them went to Israeli cities—Tel Aviv, Jaffa and smaller places—but now the number was smaller; some had been fired for observing strike days, or quit their jobs because they no longer accepted the old disease of dependency and wished to hurt Israel by giving up their menial jobs which Jews did not want.

The older men still covered their heads with the *hata*, a white cloth held in place by a ring of black braid at the crown. They had time, endless amounts of it, put out to pasture so soon while their sons did battle, refusing to lead the same squashed, humble lives. It was these men who stood like stone. They stood and stood. They willed the names of their sons to be called but it was not enough. They stared. They looked aloof.

It was a Friday and after the first two hours people wanted to be heard. They were never so cowed or bullied that they had lost the talent to complain. Some thought that the foreigner taking notes had power, no other reason for her presence came to mind, perhaps a report was to be written.

There was no rotation system for the visitors, no systematic method, no certain date when a relative would be admitted. It was haphazard and they knew it was by intent, an old tactic to exhaust and demoralize them.

"Six brothers in Ansar II—age sixteen, age seventeen, twins who are eighteen, age nineteen, and age twenty," a woman in black said, tweaking my sleeve. "They confessed they were throwing stones. The youngest"—a large worn hand went up to her face—"well, he was a healthy boy. Now he looks like a ghost. Sometimes we cannot even sleep." She was the mother who wanted to lay out all the facts. In her mind the children were growing thinner, weaker, withering from lack of good food. A man interrupted her.

"We wait and we wait. I have only seen my son once. How his face is changed in that Zionist jail. We can't expect anything. He was never sentenced. A lot of the prisoners were arrested without provocation."

There was more, he refused to be rushed although now a soldier was staring, the interpreter was nervous, others wanted to recite their own sorrows and jostled to get closer.

"When they come to take anyone it is in the middle of the night, even in pajamas! He is never given a chance to get dressed." Assuming that a foreign lady would not know the worst, he whispered: "The soldiers do awful things to the human body."

A woman elbowed in the ring of people to say that her son was seized on Omar Mukhtar Street at six A.M., the hour when most men who still work in Israel have already left. He was on his way, she said, and what harm was he doing?

That December, when it rained although the cold was not so terrible, a handsome and erect man, speaking English correctly, needed to have his say, too. He was sixty-five with numerous children. His son named Hatim was in Ansar II, it must have been a year since he was taken. The prisoner was married with three children, still small. His wife could not easily leave them so the father came every two weeks to wait it out. They all lived in section K in Jabalia Camp. It was a dreadful business.

"In nine months his wife has only seen him four times," the man said. "Only two visitors are allowed. As I told you my son was not charged. After such a long wait the visit is only for a few minutes, never more than ten. My son is twenty-four."

The rain grew persistent and there were damp splotches on his shoulders but he appeared not to notice. He wore an elegant old checked jacket with a slightly English air in the wide lapels and deep vent. A pocket had been ripped and sewn up several times quite neatly. But the jacket, once expensive, was not warm enough. He was ready to walk home when offered a lift to the edge of the camp.

He spoke again of the son, a tired man not given to surges of either hope or despair, balancing himself between the two. The ride to Jabalia was a relief and he was grateful. Leaving the car he bowed slightly and shared a last thought as calmly as if he were commenting on the weather.

"The more pressure, the greater the explosion," the father said, and went off, still holding the plastic bag whose contents had been carried back and forth so many times.

There are ten facilities in the Occupied Territories and in Israel where Gazan men were imprisoned. At the Gaza Central jail there were usually five hundred prisoners who often have long sentences. In a separate facility are rooms for interrogation by the Shin Bet where fifty to one hundred men were usually held. No less than one thousand men are at Ansar II awaiting trial or transfer. The largest prison, Ansar III, usually holds four thousand five hundred men, who may be administrative detainees or those awaiting trial or serving a sentence. Prisoners known as administrative detainees were held for a year without knowing the charges or being sentenced. The state simply invoked emergency regulations suspending the right to habeas corpus, a practice introduced by the British during their Mandate in Palestine.

Men may wait up to six months for a trial but after the first twenty-eight days of confinement a judge must renew the order of arrest. In six months the prisoner must be charged and the sentence often depends on what he has confessed to the Shin Bet while being beaten, tortured and deprived of sleep.

That is the way it was supposed to work but the military courts were so crowded that the system clogged and went berserk. The procedures for Palestinians were often seen not as just but as grotesque, a parody of all legal principles. As Glenn Frankel wrote in *The Washington Post*, reporting on the army's laxness in investigating suspicious or wrongful deaths of Palestinians: "The slowness of the investigations and the leniency of sentencing are in marked contrast to judicial proceedings against Palestinians." He noted that the army routinely demolished houses of Arabs before they are charged or tried and that prison sentences for Palestinians who threw stones were as high as three years. He quoted the U.S. State Department's human rights report for 1989 which noted that although Israeli authorities in some cases had prosecuted soldiers and Jewish settlers who killed Palestinians, "regulations were not rigorously enforced; punishments were usually lenient; and there were many cases of unjustified killing which did not result in disciplinary actions or prosecutions." In Gaza they knew all this and had the harsh facts to back it up: names, dates, cause of death and witnesses.

Estimates by the International Red Cross showed that more than sixteen thousand men in Gaza had been arrested since the intifada began in December 1987. It was not unusual for more than a thousand men in Gaza to be arrested every month although the figure dips and rises. Only six or seven hundred were rounded up in the early months of 1989 when the bad weather—the forty days, the Gazans call it—brings rain, cold and mud. The figures were not complete, the totals never perfect, and they were rapidly out-of-date.

More people were wounded each month in Gaza than on the West Bank. Army units, whose full strength was thought to be at least three thousand although this is never confirmed by the Israeli Defense Forces in Gaza, rotated every six to eight weeks. It was worse for the Gazans when a unit was leaving. On their last night on duty the soldiers were apt to be more rambunctious and violent to celebrate their departure.

Some forty thousand Palestinians in the Occupied Territories passed through Israel's penal system during the twenty years of the occupation prior to the intifada and more than a thousand hard-core activists within Israel's prisons were released simultaneously under the terms of the 1985 prisoner exchange with six hundred and fifty of them choosing to remain in the Occupied Territories, according to Ehud Ya'ari, the Middle East Affairs correspondent for Israel Television, and co-author of three books. In an article, translated into English, for *The Atlantic Monthly,* he wrote: "So deep was the mark of the prison experience on the Palestinian uprising that had it not been for Israel's 'academies,' the intifada might well have come and gone in a matter of weeks.

"Much folly on the part of many Israelis went into the making of the *intifada. . . .* For years the Israelis have

successfully met the challenge of terrorists who penetrate their borders. They are unequalled at detecting and
foiling threats to their population from without. But
their sharp sight seems to have failed them when it came
to the more serious threat posed to their security
within—from the West Bank and the Gaza Strip which
are the territories occupied by Israel since 1967. Para-
doxically the more closely they controlled the Palestinians, the more their vision was impaired, and it
diminished to near blindness regarding the tens of thousands of Palestinians who passed through the prisons.
. . . Over the years, in full view of their Israeli jailers,
Palestinian security prisoners (who are held separate
from common criminals) built an independent network
whose cohesion, intellectual verve, and rich store of experience would manifest themselves in all their power
during the Palestinian uprising.

"The uprising's Unified National Committee,
which has steered the intifada by means of periodic
handbills, is constructed along the same lines as the
special committees formed by the Palestinian security
prisoners. It embraces the principle of equal representation for all its factions, regardless of their size and standing, and of unanimous agreement rather than majority
rule. For the Palestinians these two precepts—parity
and unanimity—were born inside Israel's prisons."

But this version was disputed by some of the wisest
men in Gaza who denied that the Palestinians in Unified Leadership in Jerusalem, or in the smaller cell under
their command in Gaza, were so profoundly molded by
years in prison as the Israeli writer believed they were.
No Gazan could say much more. To admit knowing the

names of the men in Unified Leadership was a betrayal of trust and placed them in great danger.

While it was true, as Ehud Ya'ari wrote, that Palestinians learned in Israeli prisons, the writer made them sound almost like rousing summer camps where the campers clamored to be taught. What was not pictured was the deadening dreariness of daily life in a world of men who were often sick or disturbed by bleeding hemorrhoids—a common problem—ulcers and various stomach disorders. He did not describe men who were unwashed, bored, badly fed and cramped for space in tents that were stifling in the summer and freezing in the winter. Years in prison often altered men so deeply they did not easily come back to life.

The intifada was not a coup d'etat or mutiny planned in a cell or a tent. The prisons were one of many reasons for the uprising but it was not born inside them. It happened on a certain day in December when the driver of a truck lost control and Gazans believed that he killed Palestinians by intent. No higher signal came to protest, no secret strategy was at last unfolding.

Passive resistance was not a new idea promoted inside prisons and did not originate there, as Mr. Ya'ari wrote. In April 1936 the Arab Higher Committee, which was composed of representatives of all Palestine parties, called for a general strike and civil disobedience until the formation of a national government, a representative assembly, the prevention of the transfer of Arab lands to the Jews and the cessation of Jewish immigration. In the prisons, the cadre of the P.L.O. knew the past and did not devise new methods of resistance even if the old ones had once failed.

The men were what changed. In each other the
prisoners came to understand what their true history
was. Freed for the first time in their lives from the
lifelong, iron embrace of the family, all sorts of men,
jumbled together, began to see maps of their own lives
and their occupied nation more clearly. No man as-
cended above the others, or knew privilege in the group.
The dentist and the laborer, the shopkeeper and the
teacher, the street cleaner and the lawyer: all taught and
all learned in different ways. They often came to believe
that each man, even the roughest and simplest among
them, counted. All of them would count. They learned
why the occupation by Israel must end but not how to
achieve this or how to overcome the old faults.

So much love for Palestine in these forsaken places
and love for the suffering of others although, in the
manner of men everywhere, they did not use that word
to describe their closeness. For a few Gazans, prison was
an extraordinary experience if it did not last too long.

Sitting on a tufted velveteen chair at home, Dr.
Zakari Aga, a massive and magisterial man, was willing
to explain one more time how absurd it was for the
Israelis to have arrested him the year before. Many men
did not pretend to be innocent because they saw themselves at war but he kept insisting an injustice had been
done. The commanding presence of the physician—the
huge torso, the jutting jaw, the stern gaze beneath the
eyebrows that are darker than the clipped white hair—
concealed the kindness of the man. For five years, he was
Chairman of the Arab Medical Association in Gaza,
whose twelve hundred members included physicians,
pharmacists and dentists here and in several other Arab

countries. At one meeting, Dr. Aga expressed sympathy for the families of two students who were killed, one in December 1986 and the other in April 1987, since both were related to doctors in the association. As an employee on the staff of Shifa Hospital, which is run by the Civil Administration, he was not permitted to make such gestures. Someone must have reported his remarks to the authorities, probably an informer in their midst. He was fired from the hospital in August 1987 and arrested at the end of April 1988. There was no interrogation by the Shin Bet. For seven months he was in Gaza Central jail. His lawyer, the famous Tamar Peleg, filed an appeal.

"I still don't know why they imprisoned me," Dr. Aga said. "During my appeal they said I was a member of Fatah since 1971. But Tamar asked: 'If you can prove such an accusation why did you ignore him until now? What is his name in Fatah, his number?' She made a lot of noise and she is the main cause that I was kept in Gaza."

He was lucky. Raji Sourani said that the jail in Gaza, under the direction of the prison service not the military, was "a five-star hotel" compared to Ansar II and Ansar III because the prisoners could exercise, it had a canteen that sold cigarettes, chocolate, soap and shampoo, and a library. The graduates of Gaza, if they were spared interrogation, did not often shatter.

"At least prison is a natural thing and we feel those in the jail are the bravest people. I felt that this was the price of freedom and the dawn will come soon," Dr. Aga said. *The dawn will come soon:* in the poetic, old-fashioned phrase, there was always the belief that the long years of individual suffering would be added up and the final total so staggering that the Palestinians would triumph. Every moment of their ordeal would be noted in that calculation. They had only to hold on, not to lose themselves in the dark, and never be divided.

"We are willing to pay the price," the doctor said. "Those who are suffering more are insisting on going on. Our intifada was not born in a vacuum and every day people are willing to go on. Everyone is suffering, in every sector."

The words had been said by dozens of other men and women in Gaza but they had a holier note spoken in that low voice in the room of velveteen chairs and a huge white china vase of pale fake roses. His arrest had caused an uproar, he was a man of considerable distinction but an uproar did not save him. There was a demonstration by the Israeli group Peace Now and a conference of doctors, Palestinian and Israeli, issued a statement calling for his release. Tamar Peleg kept calling for him to be freed, she was not one to let up, and he thought of her as one of "the world's most wonderful people."

"We are not anti-Jews, we used to live with the Jews," he then said, pausing to make sure it was being written down. "We don't want to throw the Jews in the sea." His generation, the same class of men, often said this as if the Israelis might hear and feel safer.

All the harassment had begun years before; many Gazans were singled out long before the intifada began. In 1975 he was detained for a few months and in 1981 his travel documents rescinded so that neither the physician nor his wife were able to travel abroad. They had six children ranging in age from eighteen to six; several daughters lined up to say hello to the visitor. "Oh, they are *old* children," Dr. Aga said, smiling at the girls.

Until the final day of his incarceration Dr. Aga had no idea if he would be released for his imprisonment could have so easily been prolonged. The cell in the Gaza jail was too small as all cells are. Nine men, often more, lived in a space slightly larger than ten by ten feet. Their beds were slats of iron with very thin mattresses and blankets and when their number grew the newest arrivals slept on the floor. There was a toilet and two small windows. The prisoners ate in the cell. One hour of exercise was allowed outside the walled courtyard but this group went at a different time from all the others.

But Raji Sourani, in the same cell, who had known so much worse, thought that they were being well treated. What was so unnerving, he said, was the men who were taken out to be deported. He wondered if all of them were not on the list and if it was only a question of days.

"We were prevented from seeing other prisoners, we could not even pray together, there was no chance to mix," Dr. Aga said.

He was the oldest although only in his mid-forties. The others included lawyers, a social worker who had studied in Poland and another doctor. Some prisoners were sick and a few injured from beatings. One man had legs that barely worked because, during interrogation, a Shin Bet man had jumped on them as if he were skipping rope.

A patient man, the physician learned greater patience. In his ordinary life, so preoccupied with his prac-

tice and his family, he could not have dreamed that
there was any happiness to be found in that foul little
room. Yet it was here where he felt himself most useful
among his new friends.

"In prison I was more calm, more resigned, I felt
more at peace. Outside prison I feel I am waiting—
anyone is subject to detention," he said. That day in
Gaza he did not try to hold down the feelings that shone
on the large, strict face.

"When I left there I was very sad. It was embarrass-
ing, I wept. I left something of myself in that place. It
was the contact day and night, why I couldn't even have
that much with my own children."

In Palestine Square there was always the silhouette
of the two or three soldiers, and a submachine gun, on
the top of a building where they saw everything below:
people going in and out of the tiny shops, the merchants
talking and selling, the street vendors who possessed the
sidewalks and the swirl of old cars every morning. The
people pretended that they were free but were always on
the lookout. In the huge souk, with the Fraas market,
women went about their business, their minds on how
much the vegetables, the fruits, the spices and raw meat
would cost.

Even on the quiet days, when the world heard nothing from Gaza, a certain nastiness never let up. An
ordinary street could yield the small and ugly drama,
more proof of who was running things. One morning,
the driver of an army jeep, an ordinary vehicle not
armor-plated, was weaving through traffic as if he expected all others to yield and banged into an old green
Peugeot. The stunned Palestinian driver, holding a

handkerchief to his face where he had hit his head, was slow in getting out and looked dazed. The jeep stopped, a soldier ran over, looked at the man and said in Hebrew: "Go to a hospital." The Palestinian, bleeding only a little, seemed astonished and did not run to see the dent in his car. The jeep raced off at the same speed. The usual crowd collected around the woozy man and once more gave a verdict on how the soldiers, those dogs, drove in their streets.

In the shared taxis, called *services*, as if the name were a French noun, strangers did not talk to each other. Passengers paid their fares, very small amounts, at the start of the ride not at the end. The women in their long skirts always sat together when they could but the protocol changed if the female was foreign, bareheaded and bare-legged, eager to chat. So the science teacher with a child, who spoke English, and wanted to practice, was happy to talk about the place where he was raised and said in a sudden spurt of rapture: "I love Gaza as I love my finger—my eye—my son."

He saw beyond the garbage, the sealed entrance to the Islamic University with its empty, dusty classrooms, the new graves, the burning tires, the guns and the ugly unfinished villas not completed because of the intifada or the fall in the Jordanian dinar. He was clearly not from the camps but from a more orderly world that had for so long seemed stable and safe. He saw a different place in the pewter-colored light when the rain finally stopped and he and the boy took their leave.

III

In the Camps

THE BARBER IN BEACH CAMP, WHO GAVE SUCH GOOD haircuts in his own house, swung between grief and hate in the last days of April when, on the twenty-fifth, two of his children were shot. A daughter, who was fourteen and in the sixth grade, was sitting outside the house around five P.M. when an M-16 bullet pushed into her mouth and traveled up the left side of her nose. The parents were both busy when the shooting started and it was the wild shrieks of other children that made them rush outside. The girl was only dreaming and looking at the sky when she was hit.

"The soldier meant to kill her. Oh yes. The neighbors all thought she was dead—there were a lot of witnesses. They try to destroy us psychologically because the life of my children is very dear," he said. It was commonplace for children who had not committed any offense to be terribly punished.

He almost fainted when he saw so much blood for in his panic the father thought that the girl had been slain or that all of her face was gone. Riding in the ambulance with the girl the barber was a man gone berserk.

"The Israelis stopped the ambulance. When I saw them I felt faint. I lost my temper, I went wild. I tried to catch one of the soldiers—to beat him—but my friend stopped me. This is not a life. When the Israeli soldiers break in it is like gasoline and fire. The Palestinians are the fire."

A small wiry man with deeply lined skin and thick unruly hair, he rubbed his face a lot as he spoke. In the main room of the house there was a table, two cots, a painted cardboard armoire, tea cups on display and a vase with plastic flowers. It was jammed with children for there were fourteen in the family. Three of the girls, who were fifteen, twelve, and one-and-a-half years old, were born deaf and the parents never knew why. The wounded girl was now home with only a faint scar high on her cheek where the bullet had been removed. None of her teeth had been lost. She was quick to smile and to lean against the foreign stranger as if grateful for any embrace. Her mother said she stayed indoors nearly all the time. Everyone always thought it was the deaf girls who were in danger, not the others.

"So much suffering," said the barber, who was still morose. His eighteen-year-old son was hit on the same day as his sister but an hour earlier. The bullet tore his colon and he was taken directly to a hospital. The barber thought that his son, still in the hospital, looked terrible. To distract the brooding father I asked to see the barbershop he and some friends had built. There were a few narrow steps leading down to a basement which looked like a tiny bunker with a professional barber's chair and a mirror on the wall. Praise for his haircuts came often from a very tall American surgeon who was a volunteer at the Ahli Arab Hospital, a Jew taking out the bullets inside Palestinians. The surgeon from Boston was only known as Dr. Jay because foreign family names were too difficult for the Gazans to remember or pronounce. The American liked to say that never had his hair been cut so well and it cost less than a dollar. In that house his name was holy.

"He was there for the operation on my son," said the barber, a kindness that could never be forgotten. It was the American who had helped steady him during the weeks of worry and who said the boy would pull through. Business in the barbershop kept dropping off as fewer men could pay for haircuts. When I came back in August to see how the son was recuperating at home, the barber and the boy had more bad news to report. Last week there had been another day of death and trouble.

"I was cutting hair when there was noise and shouts. More than two hundred boys, girls, women—oh, everyone—were outside and for three hours there was a confrontation. Four to seven P.M. The soldiers came in on foot, many many of them, and they had clubs. They broke the mirror on an ambulance."

In the morning of that day the people saw how it would go. There were troops silhouetted by nine A.M. on top of a new observation post, an empty office building at one edge of the camp, and more soldiers at the main entrances of the camp bothering and blocking people wanting to leave or come in. The barber was sure that the Israelis on that day were deliberately taunting the people and were hungry for the trouble that came soon enough. It was a contradiction: the new Israeli commanding officer of the Gaza Strip, General Matan Vilnai, was believed to have issued orders for troops not to deliberately provoke the populace as the intifada went into its second year. He even ended the old practice of putting Gaza under a total curfew in the belief that collective punishment was not useful. Vilnai was clever, people said in Israel, he would manage the Arabs.

The wounded son, who had worked as a tailor in town, could not easily move or bend over or walk upright. It was time to end the conversation for he looked tired and sometimes the wounded would lose their tempers and exhaust themselves while giving their views on the occupation, on the Israeli troops. Just that morning a man who was shot in the chest and needed his rest started to yell: "The Israelis should have the new ID cards, they are in *our* country." His wife told him he must try not to talk so much.

The barber said a little more about the bullets and the clubs, just ordinary talk. In the spring the soldiers wielded the old wooden clubs like small baseball bats with black tape on the handles for a tighter grip. But these often splintered or broke on impact so nails were driven in them to prevent this. Often a Palestinian man who had been clubbed had slashes on his face and body as if cut by a dull razor blade but it was the nails. Then plastic clubs were preferred because they were more efficient. Not all the army patrols in the town carried clubs as the year went on but inside the camps the soldiers liked them.

He did not want me to go without carrying a message for his old friend who had left Gaza and was greatly missed.

"Remember us to Dr. Jay," the barber said. "Be sure to do this." Most of the children came out to inspect the car but the shot girl just stood in the doorway and waved goodbye.

On the West Bank in 1989 children accounted for 17.7 percent of the injured in the first three months of the year. But in the Gaza Strip children were 40.5 percent of the casualties in those three months and slightly over 38.3 percent for the year. And from January until the end of March the number of patients at the emergency clinics established and run by UNRWA in the eight refugee camps had increased by 67 percent from a total of two thousand nine hundred in January to four thousand eight hundred in March.

This is how it went. A delegation on a short-term consultancy for the World Health Organization composed of a Dutch social psychiatrist, a Norwegian anesthesiologist, an Irish trauma care nurse and a German reconstructive surgeon wrote a report that spring called Needs Assessment in Respect of Emergency Medical Care in the UNRWA Clinics and Non-Government Hospitals of the West Bank and Gaza. Its figures were not exhaustive, the authors pointed out. No one in Gaza read the report, which was not intended for public distribution, but the contents would hardly have been a surprise. Statistics age rapidly but the findings of the delegation, written in a grave precise language, summed up the entire year, and all that was to come.

"The types of weapons and methods of abuse of the civilian population cause a wide variety of physical and emotional damage. Physical injuries range from deadly penetrating injuries to minor bruises. One common form of ammunition is the heavy, large caliber (10 mm) steel bullets with or without a thin layer of black plastic (plastic-coated metal bullets). Depending on the distance to the victim, these steel balls may cause impression fractures of the skull, bruises, intracranial lesions or large vessels injuries, with death as a result. Bullets made of hard plastic can also penetrate the skull, thorax and other vital parts causing death. High velocity ammunition"—a reference to M-16 bullets, or live ammunition—"is used with increasing frequency. This splinters into fragments in the victim and there is no exit wound. A number of deaths caused by penetrating injuries to the brain and the heart were reported to us by doctors both in the health clinics and hospitals. . . ."

The overall age of the injured, this report said, is very low. About thirty-six percent of the intifada-related injured in Gaza were less than fifteen years old. Secondly, the report stated that injuries were distributed all over the body, and not limited to the lower extremities. "We saw extremity, head, chest and abdominal gunshot wounds and injuries from beatings," the doctors' report also said. "Tear gas used in confined areas had caused severe asphyxia, eventually leading to death especially in the youngest and oldest."

The group was not welcome in Gaza by the Israeli authorities, who refused the consultants access to Shifa Hospital.

"The lack of respect for the Geneva Convention among soldiers and officers poses a serious threat to *the security* of patients treated at UNRWA health care facilities. Injured risk not only to be arrested at or in the health centres, but may also be subject to beating and denied medical treatment. These flagrant violations of the role of health services affects also the security of nurses, doctors and other personnel. We interviewed a number of them who had been beaten, arrested, detained or shot at while performing their legal medical duties.

"Many injured will avoid UNRWA facilities due to these serious violations of international law. The initial injury and its consequences may be fatally aggravated due to the subsequent delay between the time of injury and that of proper initial and definitive diagnosis and treatment.

"Of course the Palestinians working in the health centres and emergency clinics have no extensive experience or training with war type injuries nor with the changing patient load caused by long curfew periods," the report said. There was much to be done, the delegation made clear much that was needed. Praise was also bestowed.

"The clinics are staffed with dedicated Palestinians with relatively long experience and excellent local knowledge. Professionals have high morale and have shown great courage during their difficult situation."

The psychiatrist was not able to make "systematic observations regarding the psychological and psychiatric consequences of the intifada, due to the priority of surveying the physical consequences" but offered some considerations on the psychiatric consequences of the emergency. They were: ways of coping with loss and bereavement; and the impact of family structure.

He noted a new sense of identity rising from the common suffering and sacrifice. Various coping strategies among families of the injured or disabled were apparent to the psychiatrist. The first was the Palestinian response which he called "this is our life." The second strategy was the ability of the Gazans to make death or disablement into an honor. The dead became martyrs, the cause never so clear and compelling. The death of a man in Gaza made an example of him. That such coping is bound to fail, the psychiatrist wrote, was evident in the case of a man who had lost both hands and feet and had to be cared for by his wife. The father of the amputee almost wept when describing the son's helplessness to the psychiatrist.

The intifada had shaken and changed the structure and values of the family, the psychiatrist said. He thought in a sense men were now the most vulnerable. Everyone knew this.

That year, as in the year before, the husband or father could not provide protection to his own parents, wife or children. In the eyes of Muslim men, their own immense value diminished when they were beaten in front of women and children or could not protect or rescue members of the family from attack. The man knocked to the floor and kicked was no longer the strong commanding head of the family. The arrested man, being prodded and tied up, was no longer the father who can keep harm away. It ate into some men deeply and they did not know how to relieve their own shame. Only a few sought relief in revenge as if this would redeem them.

There were always days in Gaza when the staunchest among them could not keep up the stoic pretense.

In the taxi going to the camp the driver Fah'mi, who used his uncle's car to make a living, could not conceal his melancholy. There was a reason: at eight P.M. the night before he had barely made it home in time for the curfew and soldiers stopped him in Beach Camp because he was still out. They let him off that once. But another man was caught soon after and everyone heard his voice, how he pleaded with the soldiers. It must have annoyed them.

"The fellow said he had had an argument at home and just wanted to step outside awhile," Fah'mi said in

Arabic to another passenger who spoke English. "They kept beating him. You could hear him scream and scream."

Hundreds of people had listened and not the strongest among them dared go outside to stop it. It was a beating just for the sake of beating. The driver thought the soldiers worked over the man for twenty minutes, at least, as he called out in the name of God for someone to come forward.

In the northern quarter of the town, on the coast, Beach Camp, known in Arabic as Shati Camp, is a world unto itself. Some foreigners in Gaza, whose business it is to measure such things, said Beach Camp was hardest hit during 1989 and that, proportionally, it suffered the most. There was a grim competition with the bigger Jabalia Camp, with its population over fifty-two thousand, which usually took more casualties. From December 9, 1987, when the intifada began until the end of November 1989, seven hundred and eighty-two people were shot by live ammunition in Jabalia while six hundred and sixty-one were shot in Beach Camp. In that same period, two thousand one hundred and forty persons in Beach Camp were beaten and required hospitalization or medical treatment, one hundred and fifty-six were shot by rubber bullets and two hundred and sixty-six by plastic-coated metal bullets. The largest number of people in any camp, one thousand seven hundred and eleven, suffered from the effects of tear gas during that period.

The original population of twenty-three thousand were mainly refugees who after the 1948 war came from Lydda, Jaffa, Beersheba and the southern coastal plains.

In 1950 UNRWA was created by the United Nations General Assembly to help the desperate Palestinians. By 1971, twenty-eight thousand five hundred and ninety-seven refugees were living in eight thousand two hundred and forty-four of these UNRWA built homes. In March of that year, the Israeli military under the command of Ariel Sharon demolished two thousand two hundred and sixty-three rooms that housed eight hundred and four families. One-sixth of the camp's population was left homeless. One purpose for the demolition was to widen the roads in the camp to allow easier access for military vehicles and personnel during Sharon's campaign to end armed resistance in the Gaza Strip.

"Sharon's boulevards," a Palestinian said. "That is what we call them. He brought us another reign of terror." That was the point.

"We used every kind of subterfuge," Ariel Sharon wrote in his memoirs, *Warrior*. "We infiltrated our own 'terrorists' into Gaza on a boat from Lebanon, then chased them with helicopters and search parties, hoping that eventually the real terrorists would make contact. Eventually they did. We would stop an Arab cab driver who might have been speeding, then put our own people in the car and tour the camps looking for armed terrorists who intimidated and shot Arabs going to work in Israel. We had people selling vegetables in the market, drinking coffee in the coffeehouses, riding donkeys."

Beach Camp is a huge place without sidewalks, its own market or any shops at all. There are more than forty-two thousand five hundred inhabitants on a site about one hundred and twenty-eight acres, somewhat smaller than the Mall in Washington, D.C. between the

Lincoln and Washington monuments. There was one UNRWA health center staffed with four doctors so that each doctor is expected to attend to one hundred and ten patients a day. A temporary subcenter was opened after the intifada began. There are eleven elementary schools run by UNRWA and three preparatory schools with thirty-six teachers for nearly seven thousand five hundred pupils.

Two supplemental feeding centers in the camp gave meals to nearly three thousand children, sometimes only sandwiches and fruit at noon provided the parents had registered the children at the center. No child was given food if its name was not registered. Food was also given to adults under a program called Special Hardship Cases and milk to infants and children under three years. Rations were needed by more than six thousand people. Sacks of flour were also handed out on specific days and times. Each sack weighed about one hundred and ten pounds and a family may claim two. The men, who put the sacks on one shoulder and scurried to a car, soon had a powdery paleness as if they were in disguise. Everyone was cheerful for the flour was needed so the women could make bread for every meal. Sometimes it was the meal, eaten with a few onions and salt. In the summer thirty-seven thousand two hundred and sixty sacks were handed out in Gaza and the Strip. Hunger and hardship were spreading.

At first there were only tents, then mud-brick shelters and, finally, the cement block houses built more than twenty-five years ago. The foreign delegations, visiting the camps, shuddered at the crowding, the narrow open sewers, the garbage piled outside, the children without toys or playgrounds fooling around in the sand, and were not always able to believe that these were not a fallen, disgraced people. The Gazans in the camp saw themselves, often enough, as wretched but not pitiful, persecuted but never ground down or pacified. People were surprisingly tolerant of the foreigners that kept coming to the camps to stare, to say a few words, as if these outings would someday be of good use. A visitor was always welcome in their house, coffee always offered in the poorest place.

The Israeli authorities hoped to persuade people to move out of the camps, those huge fierce concentrations of hostility and an implacable belief in their entitlement to a Palestinian state on their old land.

So Gazans were offered the right to rent for forty-nine years a patch of land, perhaps one hundred and twenty square meters, at various sites in town and on the Strip where a house could be built at their own expense. Raji Sourani said the contract, written in Hebrew for Arabs to read, specified that if a family agreed to the offer the house they inhabited in any camp would be demolished so others could not live there.

Few could afford to build but more important was the understanding that the Israelis wanted to scatter and weaken them. In the camps the Gazans were refugees with a claim. Then, too, in the camps they benefited from UNRWA's free vaccinations and clinics which prevented epidemics, schools, various distributions of food and the efforts of an organization which always tried to act, although not always successfully during the intifada, on their behalf.

"Why is your mother in tears again?" I asked a

twenty-six-year-old friend named Sobeh, which means "morning" in Arabic. He was dreaming of going to the United States, of reaching California, its heavenliness so clear in his mind. The weight and persistence of the dream made him scowl that day. He was a small man inclined to slump, with a sharp large nose and perfect, very white teeth. He had not shaved because that morning his mother did not wake him up in time, and he did not wish to hear my views anymore on a man who needed his mother to be his clock.

"Because she says that if I go away she will not know what God has written for my life," Sobeh said. The visa was never granted. Weeks later, at the U.S. Consulate in Tel Aviv, an American official decided to deny it on the grounds that he had no satisfactory address and his papers gave his nationality as "undefined." All Palestinians have "undefined" nationality marked in their travel documents; it is one more poison to swallow.

His mother was a tiny energetic woman with a small kind face shaped like a nut. A long dress concealed her arms and legs, her hair was hidden by a scarf even when she was home scrubbing. It was a worried face until she smiled and then grew younger for a few seconds. But the tears came too quickly and too often although she insisted she was not worn down and kept bustling out to the kitchen, with its two-burner stove and old refrigerator, as if there were twenty people to feed not the seven of them. There were the parents, the single sons, and the daughter of one of the oldest married boys.

"She is always busy, if I ask her something and tell her to sit, she says 'no, no, not now, I have so much to do,' " said Sobeh.

Pride flickered over the mother's face and made her shy when Sobeh was speaking English as if her own child possessed this magical gift. Here was the educated son, their treasure, who had studied at Bir Zeit University before it was forced to shut and who came home, without his degree, to help the family. Not many children from Beach Camp went to Bir Zeit and with the usual reverence of Palestinians for education the family saw in him their future. It was the third brother, Hane, at a sewing machine doing piece goods who had helped pay for that education. Many men in Gaza sewed for subcontractors to Israeli clothing manufacturers. Hane asked for nothing and said little. He kept working. At twenty-two he was the son most in danger, his thin bitter face a small record of a life that other men also loathed, which showed not only the pain of the poor but of a man in bondage. There had never been a day in his life when he had not seen Israeli soldiers. Neurotic was too foolish a word for his state of mind.

"He never finished school. He didn't pay attention as a child so he was beaten a lot, on the knuckles, palms and the soles of his feet. The children were always beaten in the schools until Unified Leadership called for a stop and said that was not permitted anymore," Sobeh said. He felt closest to Hane, both of them knew themselves to be stranded. Their lives were so askew and uncertain, the money so scarce, that they felt they could not marry. It was an absurd thought. There were two older sisters, now married, but the brothers knew nothing about women. At Bir Zeit University Sobeh hardly knew how to talk to female classmates. Intercourse with

Arab women was not permitted in Gaza until a man married.

All the vigor came from the mother for the sons were often listless and silent, sewn inside their depression that came and went. Their father, who for years worked in a citrus plant sorting oranges, seemed to have stopped speaking altogether but it had nothing to do with the intifada. He might have been ill or bored to death. At sixty he was seen as very old and nothing was required of him. It was the mother whom the sons talked to and consulted, the father did not count anymore. He did not figure in their discussions and sat by himself, staring, and would not speak of Jaffa where his family once farmed.

"My husband is so good and honest and never a man who practiced deceits," said the mother, who did not want people to have the wrong impression of the lifeless man.

She was astonished when questions were asked about her own life, the early days, for no one had ever done this. She did not know her exact age, fifty-four or fifty-five perhaps, and there was no birth certificate. She remembered hearing as a child about the Great Revolt against the British in the Mandate. It was started by a social reformer and religious teacher known even today to all Palestinians as Izz al-Din al-Qassam, who began the first guerrilla war against the British to stop their sponsorship of mounting immigration of Jews. After being killed in action, he became a national hero who inspired the Great Rebellion of 1936–1939. (In Beach Camp there was even a group named after him, the Qassam Brigade, who dressed in black and were members of the Popular Army.) The British prevailed in their Mandate: five thousand Palestinians were detained, one hundred and forty-six hanged and five thousand homes demolished.

The woman's story began at the point where it always starts for middle-aged Palestinian refugees, with the catastrophe in 1948.

"Our house in Lod had six rooms, an Israeli engineer demolished it to build his own. There was such a good garden with many kinds of roses and jasmine. My father and uncles planted the roses. There were orange trees and a grape arbor and a swing for us."

She planned to say more. Sobeh's eyes were closed as if he were trying to see the swing, the six rooms instead of the little one where we sat, so small it could be crossed in five long steps, if the couch was taken out. But he was only tired having stayed up too late watching television again. He was most beguiled by "Dynasty," as many were.

Thirty-two years later she saw the garden again. An attachment, deeper than any known to most Americans except for those of native Indian blood, pushes the Palestinians to go back to look at their land where the Israelis have lived for more than four decades. It is as if spirits were expecting their return. Sometimes the men just went to see old trees that bear fruit. In Gaza, a visitor from Jordan, staying at Marna House, explained how he went back by himself to his village near Lake Tiberias to take some olives from the trees planted by his grandfather. He was stopped and threatened by an Israeli with arrest if he stole olives. He was caught filling a jar and the olives were taken from him. But the next day he crept back to try again so that his children might taste those olives, and be wiser. It is the old story, ten thousand versions exist.

"In 1980 we visited our house," the mother of Sobeh said as if the old house still stood. "It was ten A.M. in July, at the end of the week. Near the house where Israelis live some Arab neighbors took us to see the garden. Oh, I felt my heart thump and I felt so hopeless. I had a vision of my father and mother, my sister and brothers playing. A woman came out on the stairs shouting 'Go away, go away' and others came out of that house. They were very frightened. The women were shouting so loudly and shaking their fists so we left quickly."

Her marriage in 1951 was arranged by a relative but she did not think the rest of her life would be spent in Gaza.

"My husband's family chose to stay because in two or three weeks we would go back to Lod. Today, tomorrow, soon, very soon," she said, as if to tell me what trusting souls they had been, always waiting for the right to return.

"Why did we flee Lod? We heard such stories about Deir Yassin—how a woman's breast was cut off, how the dead were not put in graves, that there were shootings. Well, it was my mother who heard all this from other women. We didn't know anything except these stories."

The name of Deir Yassin, a village near Jerusalem, where a battle and massacre took place on April 8, 1948, is a paroxysm that has recurred for forty-odd years. People still quarrel about it. This much is clear: about one hundred and twenty men from the armed Zionist groups, called the Irgun and the Lehi, who wanted to expel the British, attacked the village and going from house to house were able to kill at least one hundred and twenty Arabs, or as many as two hundred and fifty of them, display some of the corpses and parade some of the prisoners through Jerusalem. The operation was another success for the news spread through one Arab village after another, like a giant flamethrower, causing panic and huge evacuations. People ran from their own deaths or defilement. There was no military objective at Deir Yassin, only a lesson to be taught.

Deir Yassin appalled some Jews who had fled to the United States and, in a letter to *The New York Times* in December 1948, they mentioned the massacre and the "unmistakable stamp of Fascism" of the Herut party of Menachem Begin who was coming to this country to raise funds for it. Begin was the head of Irgun who after the killings, according to his biographer Eric Silver, sent a message to his troops: ". . . As in Deir Yassin, so everywhere, we will attack and smite the enemy. God, God, Thou hast chosen us for conquest." Among the twenty-eight people who signed the letter against Begin were Hannah Arendt and Albert Einstein.

It was a quiet day in Beach Camp, only the soft plop of a rifle making a noise now and then, not the sharper staccato of the M-16. "Eat, eat," said Sobeh's mother in Arabic bringing out fruit, bread and hummus and making me smile, remembering how many times Jewish women in New York had said this, urging me to eat because I looked too thin. With his mouth full, Sobeh tried to describe what their lives were like now, the four sons all living at home. The youngest was Atef, sixteen,

who was their biggest worry. A year ago, in April, there
had been a nasty time so that the mother did not even
like hearing about it again.

A neighbor came running to their house with a
warning—the soldiers were coming close to your door
now, now. The mother met the soldiers outside and said
there was no boy at home, she was alone in the house.
One of the men brought his club down on her right arm
before they moved on, wanting to snare boys. No one
had ever struck her before.

"My mind was absent. I was in shock and I hadn't
any plan at all, I was paralyzed," she said. "But they
didn't get him. Afterward my son said, 'Forgive me, my
mother. I won't do it again.' " He had been throwing
stones and rocks. There was no other way for the Gazans
to fight. The P.L.O. did not want weapons used and
there were some guns but not enough. The Palestinians
knew, too, that if they were to open fire on Israelis the
retaliation would be massive and dreadful.

In December 1988 such terrible things happened
that the mother, with her watery eyes, looked as though
she might be having another of her headaches, squinting
again as Sobeh described a single day.

"I was in front of the house smoking. It was twelve-
thirty on a Thursday afternoon and my mother was
preparing cold lamb for lunch. We were about to eat.
Five soldiers were running after boys and they broke in.
'Where is your brother? We saw him throwing stones.'
It was Atef they wanted, again."

Sobeh then took charge and denied Atef was to
blame.

"My heart was so noisy but I didn't shiver in front

of them," he said. It was his tendency to use the word "shiver" when he meant "tremble."

"My mother went into shock," he said. "She couldn't speak."

Then Hane interfered to save Atef and said to the Israelis: "Please, my brother didn't." He was kicked in the crotch and fell, saying "God damn you" in Arabic. When a soldier pointed his M-16 at the insolent fellow the mother started sobbing and covered her face. Sobeh stood between his brother and the soldier, with a command of his own: "Hane I order you to shut up." Atef was taken away and beaten so badly his brother did not at first recognize him in Shifa Hospital. It was Hane who was fined by a military court a sum equal to nearly five hundred dollars and sentenced to three and a half months in Ansar III.

The soldiers did not like journalists, had no reason to, and were not permitted to speak to them without authorization. It was in Tel Aviv where a humane and sympathetic retired officer explained that Gaza was an insulting place for soldiers to be, facing pugnacious children and adolescents, overwrought women and conspiratorial men who were unarmed but longing to kill. The hatred most soldiers felt for the Arabs did not make duty in Gaza an honorable experience, or even an engrossing one. They would rather fight armed men, he thought.

Whenever there was a clash, or soldiers rounding up men, it was agreed that Sobeh would leave me and slip away since I could not protect him and he was without a press card. He always balked at going into hospitals to speak to the wounded or the beaten, dreading it. By then he and I had swum through thirty interviews together, a hundred conversations, in Gaza and the Strip. In his own language he seemed a different person, moving in slow and happier circles.

Arabic is a language of expression not a language of information. The tedious business of journalism, so new to him, was wearying, but he did not impose his own views and persevered. Sometimes he would refuse to translate a question which seemed dangerous, only saying in a low voice—the signal of a mutiny—"This is not our business to ask." Many Gazans feared being suspected of being a collaborator if they were too nosy or too interested in the clandestine activities of others and his inclinations were always on the cautious side. Other men came from Jerusalem to Gaza to do the more intricate interviews that held the secrets.

Some days, when there were general strikes or curfews in Beach Camp, Sobeh could not leave his home and a day of work was once more lost. The telephone was in the house of a neighbor which he could not always reach if there were the smell of trouble or the real thing. His English often became bizarre when he was at last able to get to the phone and explain what had kept him pinned inside. The little communiqué often had an unintentional comic note. "It was raining bullets outside my door," Sobeh said, meaning there had been clashes or confrontations, two words used over and over for the troubles.

One calamity followed another in Beach Camp. Other things happened too. His mother sold her gold bracelet so Hane could buy two sewing machines and work at home. Once, in the late afternoon, some small boys sought refuge in their house with soldiers on their heels and the brothers were obliged to escape, too. Two went over the wall in the courtyard but Sobeh climbed in the kitchen sink and wiggled out the small window so he could get across the roofs of the closest houses. He broke the faucet with a foot and cut his hand. The broken sink was serious. It was his mother who helped them all get out and stayed put herself. The pursued children were not rounded up that day and there were always little victories of this kind.

History was on their side, the Gazans liked to say, but no one ever ventured to say that by next year, or in ten years, they would win. "Only God knows what tomorrow will bring," said one man. A fifteen-year-old boy from Jabalia Camp sang out from a bed in Shifa Hospital that a million Algerians, yes that many, had died for their freedom, that Palestinians were ready to die—it was not the moment to point out that the Algerians were armed—and he himself would be in the ranks of the fallen. The friends squeezed around his bed were elated by such bravura, the bullet wound in his thigh— the third injury—and that small face already so deeply marked and gleaming.

The psychiatrist was apt in describing as "proud" the attitude of Palestinians that their destiny was to suffer so they would suffer more and still not capitulate. In Jabalia, some refugees often called it the Camp of Vietnam, a badge of honor they awarded themselves. There was so much talk about Vietnam during the first stages of the intifada that Bob Simon of CBS filmed a woman in a camp saying: "The Americans were stronger than the Israelis and the Palestinians are stronger than the Vietnamese." Jabalia, where the intifada began, thought the world knew of its existence. Gazans knew little about the old war in Southeast Asia, only who had won, which side had triumphed over technology, jet bombers, a rich army, the best weapons. More than that did not seem to matter.

"Have you heard that slogan?" I asked a man in Jabalia, a young man who knew English and still behaved like the clever student, polishing and correcting his answer as if we were in class.

"Yes. But it should not be said that way," he answered. "You should say it like this. The Americans were stronger than the Israelis and we are *no less strong* than the Vietnamese. We do not want to show disrespect. Vietnam is the school."

The American visitor was always treated politely although asked half a dozen times why the United States gave Israel money, why it gave weapons, why it sent over the tear gas. The older men, with so little to do, had the most pointed questions for the foreigner, and were happy to have an argument.

"Why do Americans call us terrorists?" The question was asked in different ways, always with some anger or indignation and usually put by older men who had the time to address such matters. At last an answer seemed called for, and came back.

"Well, a Palestinian killed Robert Kennedy in 1968, there was the slaughter of the Israeli athletes at the Olympics in Munich, the hijacking of the TWA plane, the killing of an elderly frail American man on the *Achille Lauro*, the explosion on the Pan-American flight over Scotland which killed thirty-five American college students . . ."

"The intifada is nonviolent," said the last man to launch such a dialogue, looking sad and slightly astonished. He said those acts had nothing to do with the intifada or the P.L.O. and Gaza should not be held responsible. Then, a long speech on Abu Nidal, the leader of the Fatah Revolutionary Command, which had nothing to do with Yasir Arafat's organization. In fact, the man said, Abu Nidal hated President Arafat and the infamous Abul Abbas was a foreign agent. It did not matter that I knew all this. When a Gazan decided to teach he was not easily deterred.

Made to feel inferior, treated with contempt and cruelty, the Gazans struggled to transcend their own feelings of helplessness but that summer the restraints, the sense of common responsibility, did not hold for a twenty-six-year-old man who entered history. He was not a revolutionary, an accomplished terrorist, or a complusive murderer but rather a man who two weeks before had started a new job and whose first child, a son, was only two days old.

He did not act on impulse but according to plan, carried out at noon on July sixth, when he boarded the Egged bus number 105 which goes from Tel Aviv to Jerusalem. Near the place called Abed Gnosh he rose and throttled the driver so the vehicle was forced off the road and crashed in a ravine. The guilty man, Abdal Hadi Ghneim, suffered injuries but did not die as he intended. He acted alone, telling no one, oblivious of the promise made in November 1988 by Chairman Yasir

Arafat that the P.L.O. would renounce acts of terrorism against civilian targets. Sixteen people on the bus were killed but the death toll kept rising in the hospitals. Here was proof, in the eyes of the Israelis, that the Palestinians were not to be trusted and were terrorists, one and all.

The large family of the guilty man lived in Nuseirat Camp on the Strip, fifteen of them in one house which had been blown up by the Israelis so now their home was two Red Cross tents in a sandy, flat area by a road. Even the children looked solemn and very tired. Neither the mother, a Bedouin with a faint blue tattoo that looked like stitches in her chin, or the young wife, in black, the face almost covered, wanted to speak except through an uncle.

He summoned energy to tell the frail story. The act had come as a dreadful surprise to all of them and at first the family tried to hide it from Abdal's wife until it proved impossible. She had just given birth and they wanted to spare her.

"All of us were sad and nervous, very nervous and very sad," the uncle said. "They arrested a brother the day it happened. Well, who wouldn't be crazy?" Perhaps it was the mother who went to the tent to find the photograph of Abdal in earlier days, as if this might reveal the sweetness in the man. There was nothing to learn from the photographer's work: a lean, serious face with a neat beard and curly hair, the eyes intense but not alarming. It was hardly the face of a coarse, stupid butcher, the accomplished assassin, only a melancholy young man with a good deal on his mind.

"On Wednesday night at ten P.M. he went to the

hospital to see his wife and son," the uncle said. "He congratulated her. She asked him: 'Are you going to bring a gift for us?' He told her: 'It will be a surprise and you will hear about it.' "

There was the only clue but the happy woman had not understood it. In the glare, the baby that she held looked sickly but everyone did. His eyes were rimmed with kohl, a Bedouin custom, and the skin had a faint bluish tinge. The shock had not swollen or blurred that strong, beautiful face of the mother, the large light brown eyes were still very clear, but she looked wretched.

"On the day it happened the soldiers came with Shin Bet to search the house at four-thirty P.M. They took all the pictures except this one, even the wedding picture which was framed and hanging on the wall," the uncle said, in his doleful, precise way. "The accident was reported on the radio but his name was not released until Saturday. But women had started whispering that it was him and we tried to hide the news. The wife of her brother"—he nodded at the woman—"told her Abdal had something to do with the bus. We guessed the house would be demolished. On Sunday they did it, we had one hour to evacuate. Friends helped us take out the furniture."

The uncle wanted to fathom what had taken possession of Abdal, he struggled but kept sinking. Still it was up to him since the real father was long dead.

"The first thing, the most important, was that his friend was shot and paralyzed in December 1987. Then he was beaten during a curfew, when all of us were at home at ten A.M. one week after his marriage on September 18, 1988. It was very bad for him and he was shouting, 'Then kill me, kill me.' "

The wife stayed silent and began to jiggle the baby who was making tiny, weak noises. The beating was with sticks, the uncle said, but he meant clubs.

"The friend was Radwan, the two of them were very close. After he was shot, his cousin was coming home one day and saw Abdal sitting by a wall, crying, his face all wet," the uncle said. "But so many are hurt . . . I never thought he would do this. He is very polite, he didn't take part in the intifada." His friend, Radwan, had been eager to plunge into the intifada, to be among the first, happy that a revolt was at last underway, until the bullet severed the spine. The sight of him, those useless legs, how small and dead he looked in the wheelchair, made Abdal weep. There was no one he loved more than Radwan; all were agreed on that.

The paraplegic in Gaza is not given intensive physical rehabilitation, or counseling, because it is not available. He is not taught to see that another kind of life is still possible, that the injury might be surmounted. The paralyzed men hide in their crowded houses and wish for death.

Radwan was engaged and soon to be married, the mother reminded the uncle, but he released the woman when he was wounded.

The mother wanted to say something: it was that the neighbors had been kind and gave them cooked food.

In a last effort, the uncle tried to provide some useful information about the life of Abdal. He had gone to a vocational school and worked as a painter of cars, very good at it too. He had to sleep in Rahobat because it was too difficult to come home every night.

"He liked to hear the news at seven-thirty and then the Israeli news at nine P.M. He also liked Radio Monte Carlo at seven P.M. and then at ten-thirty," the uncle said.

It was not wise for them to be seen talking to a foreigner in their disgrace but he went on for a while, as if addressing himself.

"What he saw . . . this humiliation . . . the beating . . . the land of his father gone," the uncle said, faltering. "If he had stayed one more week he might have changed. . . ." The thin sentence of regret made the wife lower her head.

It was the mother with the blue chin and the old, leaking eyes who wanted me to enter the tents where the heat was sickening and the mattresses too close together. "This is not a life," someone else said but it was she who gave the last words: "The sand is in eyes of the children."

The Dutch psychiatrist with the patient, neat face rinsed clean of emotion might have known if Abdal had waited for a son to be born before he boarded that bus. Perhaps the Palestinian thought that the child would someday be honored by his act, that he would always exist for the boy in a heroic light and that his would not be a fate to pity or revile. When captured he said he wished he had died.

But the WHO delegation had long since gone by then. People stayed a day or two in Gaza, then the West Bank and Jerusalem drew them back, and there were schedules to keep.

In an occupied country the population is held to
new and strict standards not by the enemy but by watch-
ful people in their midst. Nowhere were the standards
as clear and unwavering as those in Gaza where more
than one hundred deaths, and numerous injuries, were
carried out in 1989 by other Palestinians who were sanctioned to do the job. In committees they decided who
was guilty of corruption, social deviance or dangerous
behavior and what the punishment should be. The informers were always people who were morally vulnerable
and even if they had no appetite for such work could be
easily coerced or blackmailed by the Israeli authorities.
It was as though a program of purification had to be
carried out under the eyes of the occupiers. Drug dealers
were considered as despicable as informers. The Israelis
made much of these deaths. Moshe Raviv, a deputy
secretary general at the Foreign Ministry, gave the expected response to the State Department's annual report in 1990 again accusing Israeli military of abusing
the human rights of Arabs in the territories. He referred
to "the growing number of Palestinians murdered by
other Palestinians" and added: "In essence, a people is
killing itself." A perverse impression that the occupation
was the only reason that the slaughter among Arabs was
not greater was constantly advanced by Israel.

The occupation, of course, was the reason. Informers were an old story to Europeans, who could remember
World War II and what they accomplished. "No occupying power . . . can administer territory by force alone,"
wrote Michael Marrus and Robert O. Paxton in their
book, *Vichy France and the Jews.* "The most brutal and
determined conqueror needs local guides and infor-

mants. Successful occupations depend heavily upon ac-
complices drawn from disaffected, sympathetic, or ambitious elements within the conquered people. In fact,
the study of the military occupation may tell one as
much about the occupied as about the conquerors."

In Gaza the informers were often recruited by
money or threats, and one of them, a man, was killed by
shovels and axes. Sometimes a bad beating, or the breaking of the bones in the hands or legs, was sufficient
warning. Some offenders were shot to death but using
weapons alerted the Israeli soldiers and silencers were
hard to come by.

Sometimes the informers carried out elaborate ruses
to trap men into revealing their allegiance to the P.L.O.
regardless of what faction they preferred. On the sixth
of August at three-thirty A.M. fifteen soldiers entered a
house in Jabalia, waking up all seven children, to seize
a man sleeping by the side of his pregnant wife. Later,
the woman, expecting the baby in six months, could
barely describe the arrest and in the middle of a sentence began to weep so terribly that some of the children
came into the room, curious. The husband's elderly and
distraught parents did not rise to comfort her again.

The man had done well working in Israel for there
was a telephone and chairs in the room but the children
were badly dressed and went without shoes, except for
the eldest who were twelve, eleven and ten.

On the third visit the woman said two things, her
mind a bit clearer. Her husband suffered from an ulcer
and did have time to take the yellow pills he needed
when they came for him. Then, he had recently received
a letter asking him to come to Jordan to pick up some

money and bring it back. He thought the letter was from the P.L.O. but it proved to be a fake. The money might have been for certain families in Jabalia but the woman was not sure about this, only that the man who handed her husband the letter was someone he knew. In a few days, the wife said, he was going to cross the Allenby bridge to carry out the mission.

"I don't know who did this," the wife said, "I never saw him." The cousins in her husband's family intended to give her small sums of money each month, perhaps fifteen dollars in all, the most they could spare. The cousins would have hunted down the informer but there was no description of him so all they did was curse.

There were not often public denunciations but in April a man was seized inside Ahli Arab Hospital where he worked in a menial job, punched and kicked and dragged off, moaning and yelling. People turned their faces away. No one came to his defense and even the doctors did not interfere. It was all done in daylight and the next day the reasons were written in black spray paint on the wall of the open courtyard inside the compound of hospital buildings where patients and visitors liked to sit and take the air. The Palestinians responsible for beating Ibrahim Abu Medare did so for the following reasons, it said.

> For drug addiction
> Because of his immoral behavior inside the hospital
> Because he was always annoying and bothering
> the female nurses in the hospital. Signed:
> Unified Leadership.

People did not want to talk about it but two or three suggested that he may have been an informer who gave the names of the wounded to the Israeli Defense Forces thereby putting them in peril. Patients with gunshot wounds did not wish to be identified or subject to military interrogations but the informer would provide such details. So many gunshot patients had been in Ahli Arab Hospital since the intifada began that a notice was posted in the emergency room: "UNRWA Emergency Slips Should be Written for Every Single Refugee Gunshot Victim and for Other Emergencies. Slips Should be Written in the Emergency Room." Because it was a private hospital the troops did not often come in.

The strike forces who execute the punishments were formed in May 1988 and were volunteers inside each camp. They called themselves the Popular Army and each political faction had its own. In Jabalia, a twenty-eight-year-old man named Hassim—who would not have dreamed of giving his full name—admitted that he was in one group. His house was particularly nice because he had painted the walls himself, the upper half in blue, the lower half in white. There was linoleum on the floor that had been washed that morning. There were no chairs, only the thin mattresses pushed up against the walls.

"Each political faction has its own strike force," Hassim said, cracking his knuckles. "There are about two hundred men for six thousand five hundred families and this is the largest camp, you know that. The first of our duties is to protect the Popular Committees, then to be ready for confrontations with the occupying forces and then to eliminate collaborators and moral deviants who will weaken and demoralize us. The concept is that we are the arms of the Unified National Leadership."

The Popular Committees in the camps, also started in the spring of 1988, were first organized to channel food supplies donated by farmers during the prolonged curfews. There was a Popular Committee for education, another for medical relief and still another for agriculture. Refugees who were fearful of going to a hospital where records were kept—although many patients did not give their real names—were helped by the medical teams, who were supplied with kits containing disinfectant, bandages, cotton, splints, painkillers and, sometimes, Mercurochrome. It was not thought that the Popular Committees knew much about emergency first aid but their presence was helpful if a man did not want to be taken out of the camp. The agricultural committees wanted families to raise rabbits, or if they had the room, to start a chicken coop. The refugees were encouraged to grow food, perhaps peppers or another vegetable, if they had a little soil by their houses. If schools were closed by the Israelis, the Popular Committee for education would teach the pupils. And it was the men in the Popular Committees who handed out the handbills from Unified Leadership in Jerusalem which were sent on a fax machine. It had to be done very secretly for possession of a leaflet meant immediate detention so none of them could be saved. Even the torn scraps were disposed of with care.

Hassim made sure that all this was clear before he went on to describe his own work.

He was a big, serious man with no remarkable features; in a crowd he would be impossible to single out. All Palestinians in Gaza wanted to tell you their life story—as if this would explain the intifada most clearly—and Hassim was not the exception. The details are always the same: mournful, harsh, sacred.

"I finished high school in 1974. My father was arrested in 1968, at the time I was twelve years old and in the sixth grade. My journey began then, my big concern was how to continue my studies and work for the family. My father was sentenced to seven years because he was affiliated with the liberation forces. He was a policeman, you see. They told my father 'You eat from the palm of our hand then you shit on it!' He never came back. We had three armies here (the Egyptians, the British, the Israelis) and the treason was on the part of the Arab countries who were against us. The Arabs used to execute Palestinian comrades at that time—"

He mentioned the name of a famous Palestinian and saw there was no recognition of the hero who had been captured by Egyptians and given a life sentence in a Cairo jail. Most Palestinians in Gaza were accustomed to the ignorance of Westerners and no one was shocked that the name of Omar Mukhtar, for example, was unfamiliar. Revered as the Arab who struggled against the Italian occupation of Libya when it had been held by the Turks, the most important and longest street in the town was named in his honor.

Hassim was aware of the criticism aroused by the killing of the Palestinian collaborators, the tainted men and women.

"We are very much aware of this issue. We have four or five sources, we do not just go out and do it. We have information from separate sources. We also make a thorough investigation and do not act on impulse. We punish only the man who confesses. Now all the drug problems are eliminated—all these phenomena have disappeared."

Selling beer, drugs and information had once been common occupations in Gaza although Islamic law prohibits the sale of alcohol and narcotics and cooperation with Israeli security forces was seen as a moral crime. "In the evenings after work, young men shoot billiards in smoky pool rooms where hashish is often sold and where Arab informers for Israeli intelligence ply their trade," David Shipler wrote in *The New York Times* in 1981. Some Palestinians, he noted, believed that the Israeli military authorities in those years did nothing to curtail the sale of drugs because in the words of an Israeli general in Gaza "usually drugs and cooperation with intelligence agencies go together."

None of the leaflets of Unified Leadership ordered reprisals and when the number of killings rose in 1989, giving rise to considerable criticism of the Palestinians, a new leaflet called upon the people not to execute any collaborator without a central decision made by the Supreme Leadership or "without the existence of a national consensus about him and not before he will be warned and given the chance of repenting."

Attention was not paid by the local groups, who continued purging the Palestinians working for Shin Bet or those who were ordinary *jawasis*—spies who sold information.

In their attempts to explain the reprisals, some

Palestinians made clear that the deaths showed that Israel could not defend its own agents and that throughout history collaborators in countries under occupation were killed or punished. Jonathan Kuttab, a civil rights lawyer, wrote in *The Jerusalem Post:* "The population involved in the intifada is physically endangered by many collaborators, most of whom carry guns issued by the Israeli authorities and use them on fellow Palestinians and others. They provide the authorities with information that jeopardizes the lives, liberty and property of the general public." There were no jails where such collaborators could be incarcerated, he noted. And there was no court system where they could be tried.

"Resistance to occupation is a legitimate right for all peoples. It is a right in which the Soviets, the Europeans, the Americans and the entire world believe," P.L.O. Executive Committee member Mohammed Milhim said, in December 1989. He said the ratio of collaborators in relation to the Palestinian population in the Occupied Territories is "less than in the case of any other people who have lived under occupation." By September, thirty-four Palestinians in Gaza and the Strip were believed to have been killed as collaborators. Of four hundred and sixty-three attacks in the territories, two hundred and ninety-four were carried out in the Gaza Strip. "Weapons given to collaborators are issued strictly for self-defense," an I.D.F. spokesman said in the Israeli newspaper *Ha'aretz.*

"It has been normal practice throughout history to detect collaborators and execute them. I'm not saying this is the correct thing to do. I'm saying this is the *normal* thing to do." This was the comment of a West Bank professor of philosophy, Sari Nussibeh, a well-known supporter of the P.L.O.

Anxious to enlighten those who were drawing parallels between the intifada and the armed struggle of the Jews to create their own state so many years before, an Israeli reader of *The Jerusalem Post* quoted Menachem Begin in his own letter to the editor. He made use of Begin's recollections in his book, *The Revolt, The Story of the Irgun,* in which the man who had headed these fighters wrote: "A fighting underground has its own laws, one of which is that the informer will pay with his life."

But Begin defied the law, the letter said, and the decision was made not to take reprisals "which ran counter to the very spirit of natural resistance." Those who proposed the policy did not and could not produce logical arguments. "They were moved by faith," Begin wrote.

It was not a faith that touched the Palestinians, who saw themselves as murdering evil and went on with it.

That was the summer when the Popular Committees and the Popular Armies faced a new task which kept them so busy that their usual activities had to be suspended for a while. The Israeli authorities, seeking a greater degree of control over the mutinous Gazans, announced a new requirement for men over sixteen who went to jobs in Israel. They would need a new computer-coded ID card which had a magnetic strip and the old ID cards would be useless. The Gazans, in an uproar, called it the magnetic ID card. "Like your American Express card," a teacher said. "Don't leave home without it." It would not be issued to any man with a criminal record, who owed taxes or was suspected of being a political subversive. In mid-May Defense Minister Yitzhak Rabin made clear that it was a privilege for Palestinians to work in Israel, not an automatic right and that the privilege could be taken away. In Gaza men had jobs in half a dozen Israeli cities or towns, some with regular employment and others as day laborers who were selected to work by Israeli foremen or middlemen. No one knew their precise numbers. The Arabs swept streets, emptied garbage, worked in factories, cleaned hotels, helped construct Jewish homes and buildings, and saw themselves as servants, no more than shadows.

It was apparent, as Glenn Frankel wrote in *The Washington Post*, that the intifada "disrupted virtually all of the old accommodations between Jews and Arabs, rulers and subjects." Locked in a suspicious, deep embrace, the men often hated and needed each other. When curfew restrictions were imposed on the Gaza Strip it also applied to Gazans working in Israel, who had to stay home on those days. Many men left their jobs hoping to strangle the economy of Israel or were fired by their employers who complained their attendance was too spotty because they observed the curfews or general strikes called by Unified Leadership or Hamas, the Muslim Brotherhood. Or perhaps in the factories they suddenly feared what sabotage workers might carry out.

When word of the new magnetic ID card circulated, men in the camps began to bicker and dispute each other. One complained that the Palestinians in the West Bank were not required to have the card so the noose was just tightening for them and this was not fair. Dozens of men, in loud voices, swore their refusal to get the cards but then relented and did. But when the strike forces began to circulate in the camps, collecting the new ID cards, there was little resistance. Each card cost a man slightly more than ten dollars, an amount larger than what most Gazans earned for a day's work in Israel. The leaflets of Unified Leadership called for all Gazans to defy the occupiers, to stand together, to refuse to comply. It was an order not a suggestion. No one could leave without the army inspecting their identity cards at Erez checkpoint, a five-lane highway choked with cars and buses taking the men to work before the first light.

Each day the new ID cards were taken away as the Popular Armies or the Popular Committees went from house to house. They went out in the late afternoon or at night, creeping like sappers in the dark, and no one refused them entrance.

"First of all we do not force," Hassim said. "The workers give them back by themselves. They know how serious the implications are. We say: 'Do you want to go to Israel and forget the people all around you or will you stand with the people?'"

Some sulked, some sighed and all gave the cards back. But the Israelis made it possible for a second card to be obtained if the first one was "lost" and the fee was much smaller. In time most Gazan males relented, the new cards were essential if they did not want to be sealed in.

"I'm not worried, I consider this a form of political bankruptcy among the Israelis. Every day they show that they are in a state of total confusion. They don't know how to handle us, how to control us," Hassim said. "And then as long as the target of everything we do is against the occupation we have a popular base. And I, I can never retreat, my heart never stops to beat. I always long for Palestine and our own state."

Since men in Jabalia only owned one pair of sneakers when the Popular Army moved about they had to cover their feet with plastic bags so no informer could trace their identity. It changed their way of walking. They did not hide their faces with *keffiyehs*, but put on masks of stretch material. After locking the door, and covering the window, Hassim put on his own mask with slits for the eyes. In the darkened room he was now a menacing and cruel figure.

"You must scare the younger children," I said. The idea seemed preposterous to him and even the interpreter smiled. Jabalia was only a collection of villages, the children knew everything.

"The kids are happy to see us. They run with us and keep a lookout," he said. Hassim knew his life was at risk but he could not bear being apart from the intifada. The killing of collaborators was a job for the most steadfast and loyal.

By the end of the summer the Israeli Defense Minister Yitzhak Rabin, who had earlier announced his "iron fist" policy to crush the intifada once and for all, made it known that troops would now be free to use live ammunition on masked men who resisted arrest. There was a long worker's strike called by Unified Leadership to protest the new ID cards and tempers flared. The campaign to intensify resistance weakened and then ended as more Gazans gave in. It was seen as a serious failure of strategy, or even common sense, on the part of Unified Leadership to expect so many men to give up their only employment while offering no alternative. You could not, after all, raise goats or chickens, or have a large garden, in Jabalia or Beach camps although it was possible in the camps on the Strip. There were no jobs at the 7-Up plant or at UNRWA for all those who needed them. There was grumbling but Gazans stayed loyal and did not say who had failed them.

In a world they saw as so brazenly unjust, and often so insulting, the Palestinians went on with their lives. No one seemed too weary, or discouraged, to discuss it so one morning at five A.M., driving to Tel Aviv in an old Peugeot taxi crammed with seven men, all of them wanting more sleep, a twenty-four-year-old painter gave his views about the Israeli who once employed him and had called him back to work for a day. He needed the wages.

"I sometimes feel that he is not a good man, not fair. He calls when he needs me—'come on, come on, there's work'—but he would hire a man for less money and cancel me if he could. He pays the Israeli workers much better. But I am faster and much better—the Jews can do only one room a day, I can do two rooms. I did ask for more money once and he said, 'If you don't like it then leave.' Then the intifada created a kind of fear among the bosses and I stayed home for seven months. All our days were the intifada."

The supplementary feeding centers in the camps grew busier. In Beach Camp a kitchen worker said that before the uprising the children ate their food seated at little tables but there were too many of them now for such a refinement. That day they lined up for corned beef sandwiches—the canned meat came from France—on pita bread and a small clump of grapes. The children were patient and uncomplaining, it was a few grown-ups who wailed, argued, shouted and made a rumpus because of UNRWA regulations that each child's name be recorded on a card, or the fact that a mother could not take the food out without her offspring or use the card of a neighbor.

"We are seeing the beginning of hunger," the kitchen worker said. "From the healthy to the malnourished."

Someone else said the sandwich had six hundred calories and twenty grams of protein. Over one thousand children came to this center every day, walking by themselves or with others in their families. The center opened at eight A.M. and shut at half past twelve.

The children took their sandwiches home, sometimes taking a bite before they began the walk back.

"No, three of us will divide," a ten-year-old girl said when asked if the sandwich was just for her.

All the food allotted for the day was almost gone and it was not yet eleven A.M.

On some summer days it was almost normal in one of the Health Clinics in Beach Camp for the soldiers were calmer. In July in Beach Camp only twenty-one people were shot by live ammunition and thirty-one by plastic-coated metal bullets; in August twenty-two people by live rounds and sixty-four by plastic-coated metal bullets so the war was much smaller for a little while. In two separate structures, each room the size of a small trailer, a tall doctor and a male nurse swiftly examined their patients. There was a man in some pain who had been stung by a jellyfish while swimming in the sea but the patients were mostly women with ailing infants who had ear infections or fevers or respiratory problems. The ambulance driver sat outside on a bench, pleased to be so peaceful, and freed his huge feet from their sandals. There was a lull before the women began flooding in so the doctor, who trained in Cairo, was moved to summarize the history of Palestinian suffering by reciting the famous poem by Mahmoud Darwish, called "Identity Card," which many Gazan men know by heart. Sobeh knew all the lines and murmured them as the doctor went on.

When their voices died down the doctor decided something else was needed, a cruel flourish to retaliate for the aid and military assistance given to Israel by the United States for he had seen enough of its results. The words seemed dredged from the 1960s.

"America is the plague and the plague is America," he said, fixing a stern glare. He had the eyes, the nose and the jaw of the actor Anthony Quinn and was not in a good temper that day. The nurse had other things to say and his was the one conversation that had nothing to do with lost land or exile or the demented past. He wanted to discuss the effects of the tear gas made in Pennsylvania in case I did not understand how awful it was.

"Forty times I am inhaling this tear gas, close inhalation too. Now my larynx is chronically inflamed, of course I must never smoke. I have acute rhinitis and I can't sleep at night. I have this severe allergy to tear gas and no one knows what will be the later complications," he said, crossly. "I am twenty-seven and after five or ten years we don't know what happens." Sometimes taking cold water with some local very hot pepper helped but he still had to have injections.

Later, two men shot by rubber bullets came in to have their injuries evaluated. One had a fracture in the right arm, the second a leg wound that was so deep the opening seemed the size of a child's finger.

"He never went to the hospital, people told him not to bother so he risked getting gangrene and had a tetanus shot almost too late," the doctor said. The patient rolled his eyes and grimaced but did not yell or whimper when the other man fiddled with the leg.

"He has to bear it, he is a man," the doctor said, wanting me to learn something.

Casualties in 1989 in Gaza and the Strip

	Shot by Live Rounds	Beaten	Shot by Rubber Bullets	Shot by Plastic-Coated Metal Bullets	Tear Gas	Fatalities
DECEMBER	437	760	—	255	172	11
NOVEMBER	221	615	5	184	118	1
OCTOBER	226	876	11	256	188	10
SEPTEMBER	392	998	27	345	301	7
AUGUST	294	1,074	45	366	243	14
JULY	334	1,021	45	250	420	17
JUNE	233	826	35	148	428	13
MAY	552	1,230	105	326	530	19
APRIL	399	807	61	187	188	8
MARCH	274	1,257	14	107	212	12
FEBRUARY	166	803	40	163	131	6
JANUARY	251	598	22	151	224	6
TOTALS	3,779	10,865	410	2,738	3,155	124

The casualties were largely registered refugees in the camps but include residents of towns. In June, in the town of Gaza, 60 residents were injured while 335 refugees were casualties. Some injuries did not fall into one of the five categories. For example, in October, a five-year-old girl from Beit Hanoun was hit by a tear gas canister thrown by an I.D.F. soldier and suffered burns to face and chest. Figures were compiled by UNRWA from records at the Health Centers and hospital admissions.

Thirty-eight percent of the year's casualties were children under fifteen. UNRWA divided the children into age groups 1–5, 6–10 and 11–15, by sexes. Shot by live rounds in 1989: 1,506 children of whom 33 were five or younger. Beatings were the greatest cause of injuries in all the age groups with boys the higher percentage, in the 11–15 group.

IV

Women, Children
and Others

THE SOLDIERS GRUMBLED ABOUT THE WOMEN IN Gaza and the Strip as if they were not behaving nicely and often grew quite heated about it. Surprised by their own surges of boldness, the women were not the serfs that Westerners often imagine inhabit each Muslim society. No one could describe them as drowsy little worms. In Gaza they were coming to life in the insurrection, while appearing to be the same in many ways: concealing their bodies and hair, staying home to take care of others, and walking as sedately as ever in the streets. But many were transformed: unforgiving of the soldiers, refusing to keep quiet about such trespasses, such injustice. Often when a man, child or husband was arrested women wept off and on for days but this was expected and consolation of little use. Some saw how their fury and sorrow was altering them while they went on making meals and trying to keep children clean. When their husbands or sons were taken away, when their houses were destroyed or the doors kicked down during the hours of sleep, when the children were put in peril, they did not see it as the Will of God. Sometimes when the Israelis came to seize a man, they began to holler or scratch or flail but were easily overcome.

The young soldiers, who did the dirty work, did not know much about an old war in North Africa in which Muslim women, once veiled and reclusive, were recruited to be guerrillas and fought as well as the men against the French. It was Algerian women who carried explosives and planted them in two French cafes in Algiers. Gazan men would sometimes refer to that war, which the Algerians won in 1962 after eight years of struggle, but the women, more isolated and less educated, did not speak of such matters. They were not called upon to rise up but often devised different ways of helping the resistance. With so many men in prison, women began to learn how to fend for themselves, a momentous change, although there were always relatives to help them if they could.

Many Israelis thought that it was the fault of the Palestinians that women and children were being injured and a letter published in *The Jerusalem Post* voiced one man's disgust and deep unease. "The world is easily fooled while it postulates its spurious morality narrowly spotlighting our actions when it should voice contempt at Arabs who force their women and children to demonstrate. But such cynical respect for life and limb are not our way and I didn't emigrate to Israel to have my children shoot live bullets at women and children. If that is the price of our policy then I want no part of it."

There were never reports of rape only of other offenses. Centuries of modesty, enforced by their religion and the strictness of Muslim men, disappeared when women wanted to prove what had been done to them. In the women's ward at Shifa Hospital, some who had never revealed their arms or legs in public thought nothing of pulling up their hospital gowns to expose immense bruises darkening their stomachs and thighs and it did not matter if a man was looking. Bullet wounds were covered by bandages, sometimes stained, so the bruises were more shocking. One night a young Japanese who had just arrived with a delegation from Tokyo went to the hospital with me. A woman in bed, her hair tangled, called out. She wanted us to see her stomach and bared it. We stared at the vast old discolored belly as if it were a demonic painting and the Japanese boy, aghast, had to turn his head. Someone always spoke patches of English so another woman helped explain the old story told so many times in that ward. A son was seized at home so the woman tried to hold the arm of the soldier, pleading, weeping and yelling when she was knocked down and kicked, more than once. In the fall the left arm was broken. The next day going back with a gift of grapes there was a different woman in her bed with a gunshot wound. Families often came to take home a patient as soon as possible. Although the staff was Palestinian the hospital was run by the enemy and no one thought it a healthy place to recover.

In the camps the women told each other war stories and waited for the worst.

The soldiers did not fear the women, who were a pitiful match for them, but perhaps they dreaded the agitation and commotion, and were made strangely nervous. Their roughness was seen as cowardly if not despicable but armies do not ask troops to be merciful or just and there is no regulation that troublesome women be spared although the Israeli Defense Forces maintained the pretense that consideration was always given.

But the witness knew better. Once, coming back from Tel Aviv, the taxi passed the compound of Gaza Central jail where there was a ruckus on the other side of the street. The taxi stopped so the foreigner could get out and watch a group of middle-aged women, their bodies shaped like old pillows, another choir of grief. They wailed and shouted and lifted their hands as if both demanding and pleading for a small act of decency.

There were only six or seven of them making such a noise. Then the open lorry came out and passed us with the soldiers and their captives in back, the blindfolded Palestinians, wrists tied behind them. Their thick, strong hair and thin necks showed they were still adolescents. The women called out to their sons but this only elated the soldiers, who began to clap and hoot to show their pleasure in having prisoners. A big man kept jabbing a finger in the air to insult the women, a greater offense in a Muslim society than in our own. When the truck was gone, the women with their wet faces were unsure of what to do.

It seemed a good idea to stand there for a while as if that might keep them from harm. Then harm came: seven or eight soldiers, bareheaded and armed, racing out of the compound toward us in the long easy steps of the young. What was so startling was again the look on their faces, a high glee, as if now they were playing a favorite game and certain to win. The officer leading the charge saw me hissing at the women: run-run-run. In their cheap, flat sandals and long skirts they did their best, scurrying to a small side street but were too slow. The officer stopped in front of me while the troops kept running as if what he did was none of their business. The younger officers often seemed without influence on the troops as if they did not expect to be obeyed. I hoped to distract all of them, to slow them down for a bit by blocking their way so the women might have a head start.

"Tell the women—" the red-haired lieutenant said, as if I spoke fluent Arabic and might magically catch up with them. His face was nice, the eyes very green in that light. He was a bit breathless, not from running, from the suddenness of the little pursuit. He kept standing there as if not eager to join the hunt or able to stop it either. There were always the sentimental and sad moments in Gaza when, looking at an Israeli, I thought how he might have been a friend in another place, another time, how his own history and traditions deeply joined us, that his mother might be like old friends at home named Miriam and Esther. But that was finished now, fear was more important. Then the lieutenant began catching up with his men and I went to the taxi still waiting around the corner. The streets were silent because the shops were shut at noon and no one was walking about. In the distance there rose a faint sound, a single shriek, but the driver swore that he heard nothing and took me back to Marna House.

Yet there was a woman in Gaza who did inspire a degree of guilt, of great uneasiness, in the hearts of men when she appeared in the military courts on various offenses. Judges did not relish the sight: here was an unrepentant patriot of Palestine, a zealot, who happened to be a tiny, erect, sharp-witted old woman with a black velvet ribbon around her head keeping the snow white hair smooth, its bun never wispy. She was not afraid of judges, the Shin Bet, the generals, the troops, the police. In addition, the accused woman possessed such a ferocious and scornful glare that it might have been she who was sentencing these stupid men.

Yusra Barbari, who never married, which in Gaza was a death sentence for ordinary women, was in her mid-sixties but looked a decade older. It was an important advantage. She only wore black skirts, blouses and sweaters, even her stockings were always black, the uniform of a woman bearing a terrible loss and in this case it was a country. Once a teacher and educator she headed the Palestine Women's Union on Althawra Street where there was a nursery and kindergarten.

Founded in 1964, its goals were noble and considered shocking by some. The Palestine Women's Union intended to assist working women to achieve "equality with men in public life," to help provide "an honorable life" for needy women and orphans, to lessen the economic dependency of women by sewing, knitting, crocheting and embroidery workshops, with classes in sewing and dressmaking. It intended to contribute to the building of mosques, to bestow scholarships, but the intifada slowed things down for people were poorer and distracted by so much danger and disorder. A moratorium was imposed which Yusra Barbari ignored.

Her other mission was to speak out and once, when asked how often she had addressed people or been interviewed, she briefly reflected and said: "Since 1963, at least five thousand times, perhaps more." Her English was good. In speeches, interviews, discourses and little briefings for delegations the clear and gruff little voice repeated over and over the history of Palestine and all the treacheries and wounds. People not ordinarily inclined to graceful manners quickly rose from their seats when she appeared and often bowed slightly when she held out her hand. Foreigners were not used to meeting Arab women of superior strengths and often showed admiration as she went on with her consecrated work. The Americans tended to say that she had real class. Smaller than others, she loomed larger.

Four times in military courts she spoke her mind and it was soon apparent that she was not a dear little thing, easily dismissed. No one, not even the most calloused, wished to send her to jail, a woman of that age, weighing less than ninety pounds. Her offense in 1981 was running an announcement in *Al-Quds* newspaper that two new courses—in sewing and English—would start at the Palestine Women's Union and that teachers were needed. Summoned, she was fingerprinted by the police, "as a mafia, a criminal" might be, Miss Barbari said scowling.

"The judge was really ashamed. He told the prosecutor 'Don't you think this is nonsense?' " she recalled, unsmiling. "He said 'Do you think if these women want to take sewing they need permission from you?' The prosecutor said that a local organization cannot execute such an act without approval." Later, although not given to complimenting Israelis she said of that judge he "was a little bit decent and wise."

Then there was the matter of the map of Palestine hanging in the library of their center and the displayed Palestinian flag, both serious violations even before the 1987 uprising. Since the occupation both acts were considered criminal. Again she was fingerprinted at the police station: "But you already did this—do you think my fingerprints change?" Orders, they said, as policemen always do.

The old rare map of Palestine was very precious to her, a shrine. "It shows all of Palestine in 1948, all the small villages that are destroyed and even the names of the very small ones that aren't known anymore. The names are now Jewish. They don't want us to know our land. But here, in spite of all they have done, people still give some small names—the places where their families are from."

She gave her own defense in court and filled the room.

"There is no power on the surface of the world that can prevent me from hanging the map of my country on the soil of my mother country. The occupation is illegal and a violation of international law and the U.N. charter and the Geneva Convention of 1949." She was perfectly prepared to recite chapter and verse but was no doubt discouraged. The judge spoke English and saw his dilemma most clearly. She remembered his saying: "My lady I can't leave the court without giving you a sentence. If you were in the West Bank you would go to prison."

He proposed a fine, the way out. "I'll not pay a fine," Yusra Barbari told him. "It's not the amount of the fine, it is the fine itself." She glowered.

"She'll pay the fine," said her lawyer, a distinguished Gazan who, in the end, paid it himself because she would not. As for the flag she told the judge that it was seen on Israeli television, sold in Jerusalem and inside the Green Line so possession was hardly illegal.

Yet another day in court was required after she was quoted in a bulletin published by the Gaza Medical Society on social problems and possible remedies. It did not occur to her to rein in, to resort to nuances.

It was entirely predictable that Yusra Barbari would blame the villainy of the occupation as the cause of various societal disorders and there was only one solution: evacuation of the occupiers and the creation of a

Palestinian state under the sole legitimate representation of the P.L.O. It was the old litany heard from a thousand mouths again and again. Once more she had hurled herself into trouble. But the date of her trial was "frozen," she said, because the Governor General of Gaza cited her age and various cultural activities as considerations. Such leniency was unusual.

Sometimes foreigners were startled by how much she knew and the questions she often put to them. Why, for example, had many Americans regarded the Contras in Nicaragua as freedom fighters yet saw the Palestinians as terrorists? She often liked to bring up the Boston Tea Party with Americans, reminding them of the hallowed battle cry, No Taxation Without Representation, although the world grew deaf, she said, when the Palestinians made the same demand.

"Nobody believes that I am from Gaza, they think that Gaza is a backward city," said Miss Barbari. It was true, in fact Gaza was not considered a city at all.

Born in 1923, she was delivered by an estimable Jewish midwife who often was summoned by Arabs. The father was a middle-class factory owner, the passionate patriot who feared for his country after the Balfour Declaration of 1917 which pledged British support for the Zionist campaign to establish a Jewish national home in Palestine. Although illiterate, the mother understood the danger and what all of them must do. There were five sisters and four brothers raised in a house in the old quarter, Daraj. The children grew up attuned to rumor, turmoil, panic, fury and casualties as the Arabs attempted to thwart the British although some always thought they were only bluffing and would never relinquish the Mandate. There was no single opinion among Palestinians, only delusions and fierce hopes, defiant students and the schoolgirls with bright sashes which bestowed an air of moral mastery.

"I remember that when I was four years old that girls and women met in my father's house. They had white sashes saying 'Help the Families of the Martyrs' and they gave me the box for collecting the money. I wore a black apron. All the family put the love of Palestine in our blood." Each year there was more to do and at twelve she took part in schoolgirls' demonstrations during the great strike; an older sister even made a speech at a gathering. There were always meetings at which Palestinians would denounce the Balfour Declaration, and call for it to be annulled. An older brother, a lawyer, was shot to death by the Israelis in June 1967 going to prayer at the mosque and his body never returned. She thought the behavior of Israelis was indecent.

"They think their blood is precious, royal, and that the blood of all others is—cheap," said Miss Barbari. Two of her brothers studied in southern California to be electrical engineers and stayed on there but all of them were dead, the last dying in Gaza where he lived with his sisters and whose room was kept just as if he might return to them. She was in mourning for him too.

The Barbari girls were not raised just to be handed over in marriage for each one was educated to an unusual degree for that era. Her father sent Yusra to Schmidt's Girls College in Jerusalem for five years where she learned German and excelled in French. She believed herself to be the first Palestinian woman to ever study at the University of Cairo where she graduated in 1949. She was very clever in physics and mathematics, Miss Barbari confided, but these were not professions for women so she trained in Gaza as a teacher, was a principal at a university for women, then an inspector of a girls' school. In 1963 when Arab League countries invited a group of Palestinians to come to the United Nations to make known their views she went and felt the U.N. lacking.

"Since 1950 the United Nations was only considering the refugee problem not the political problem of Palestine, not the problem of a nation that was robbed and made to evacuate its land by force, terror and massacre," she said. Sometimes her voice flared as if she was saying that sentence for the first time.

It was a grueling three months and she was not the first Arab to feel that New York was unlovable, reminding her as it often did of Tel Aviv. That November most of the Palestinians wept on learning of the murder of the young president, John F. Kennedy, and some were even persuaded that Mossad, Israel's CIA, might have had a hand in his death. Hammered by their own history and loss they did not know how to relinquish the obsession that Israel plotted and managed everything, even such a death.

In New York she began to speak her mind. Long ago Yusra Barbari decided that every wall really was a door. But some doors jammed and others led into alleys. But there was her duty, arduous and never-ending. For more than two and a half decades she headed the Palestine Women's Union, giving up her career in education because it meant working under the Israeli authorities.

After December 1987 there were fewer children enrolled in the kindergarten because people could no longer manage the tiny fee, or because of curfews and strike
days. The sewing centers went on, and other classes.
Packages of foodstuffs were distributed to the wives of
long-term political prisoners, some blankets and sweaters were given out. Yusra Barbari tried to make money
for the center by selling the pristine works of art made
by the women: embroidered tablecloths and runners and
doilies with the exquisite little stitches in color and the
edges hem-stitched. They were always of very white
linen which looked so pure and immaculate it was hard
to imagine them in the dirty cities of America and
Europe, to be spotted by ketchup or mustard on dining
room tables, or covering bureaus where they would turn
gray soon enough from the grime that crept in. There
were the long embroidered dresses, too, but busy women
from distant places did not dress for dinner in works of
art. Alya Shawa often wore one of the long embroidered
Palestinian dresses but sales were never encouraging.
First there had to be fittings then weeks for the dresses
to be finished. The foreign delegations could not wait or
could not pay, what they might have bought were a set
of small place mats or knee-length skirts but Yusra Barbari was not interested in having these made.

Her own standards of cleanliness were almost alarming. A sister made known, only half humorously, that the
garbage pail with the lid, kept outside, was washed,
almost boiled every day. The villa where four of the
sisters lived, one gravely ill, was spotless and any visitor
who washed her hands instinctively knew the sink must
somehow be wiped and the soap rinsed off so it would

not leave a smear. The standards, set by her, were very high. In the town of litter—even in the hotel garden there were often soda cans or candy wrappers or the cellophane from cigarettes—she could not tolerate a microscopic mess. She could always be seen walking to and fro, to the center and back, to Marna House and back, a stern and elegant figure with a measured and youthful gait as if a tutor to a royal family had once instructed her when very young.

Despite her love for the father and the dead brothers and a respect for slain and captive Palestinians, she had proved she could struggle on her own, get things done, keep aloft the flag.

"We don't deal with men," Miss Barbari said, speaking of the center. "We are not in need of men. We have many efficient people so why do we need men?" Then, the afterthought: "Of course we do not distinguish between men and women as long as they are needing."

Other women, less educated and less worldly, showed the same impetus when unthinkable things happened and they were on their own. Shortly after midnight on August first, a thirty-year-old midwife named Fatmah was on night duty in the maternity ward of the UNRWA clinic in Khan Younis, a small town and a refugee camp near the border with Egypt. Four women, who had given birth, were asleep in a small ward, their swaddled infants in cribs covered with mosquito netting at the foot of the beds. There was an insistent heavy knocking on the door to the maternity section of the one-story clinic inside a compound whose patients during the day were nearly all women and babies. The knocking was so loud and strong that Fatmah made haste to open the door believing it was a patient, an anxious husband bringing in his wife.

Israeli soldiers stormed in, commandos on an urgent mission. Fatmah, with seven years of experience, was accomplished in a crisis and held her ground. There were only ten high, narrow little beds, with clean sheets and green and white blankets, in the ward, hardly a place to hide. One woman, only eighteen, was in labor but not yet ready to deliver in a room by herself. Two weeks later Fatmah was calm in her recital of that nasty night but still looked perturbed. A carpenter was working to repair more than a dozen doors kicked in by the soldiers. There was relief that a sterilizer in the delivery room, an expensive piece of equipment for the clinic, had not been broken since it stood by a damaged door.

As in any Islamic society it is prohibited—and unthinkable—for a male to be present when a woman is in labor or gives birth.

"I was really shocked," she said, in Arabic, speaking with deliberation. "But I tried to protect the women in bed who were so agitated. The soldiers searched everywhere, in the closets, under the beds. I asked one of them: 'What is it you want?' He just looked at me. A lot of them went into the delivery room and they kept kicking down the doors."

She thought there may have been as many as twenty Israelis but could not be sure in the turmoil.

"The woman who was in labor was undressed and she had been screaming but when she saw these men, the soldiers, she grew more frenzied and screamed more and more. At that moment I was terrified because I was so afraid for her. It was her first baby, too," the midwife said. The woman wore one of the clinic's robes but was still considered unclothed.

Looking back, Fatmah thought the woman yelled and shrieked so much it may have even speeded up the birth. The child came two hours later.

"The soldiers ordered us not to move or speak. They were laughing when they left here. They went into all the rooms knocking in the doors. The noise! They wanted to know if there were any boys—*boys here!*—so they kept searching all the rooms.

"I tried to call for help, and I was astonished to find the telephone line cut."

The only man on the premises was the night watchman, who sat outside, so he was arrested and two weeks later it was still not known where the fellow was being held, and why.

It was only by chance that the break-in by the I.D.F. was revealed for there was a different reason for going to the clinic in Khan Younis. It was to find a small boy who had been badly beaten by soldiers and could not speak no matter how the doctors and nurses coaxed him for his name. A new Refugee Affairs Officer, a European who had just taken up his job at UNRWA, was overheard talking about the child in the garden at Marna House, how he had seen the boy's back which led him to think the furious beating went on for quite some time. He was new to this and sounded aghast telling Alya.

The boy was gone from the clinic but the Palestinian doctor, the busiest of men, remembered the case with sorrow. Some children were throwing stones but this boy was caught and made to pay although the doctor thought it impossible that he was guilty.

"He was six or seven and brutally beaten on his back," the physician said, wanting to speak English just to be sure a sweeter version would not come to me.

"He was in shock, perhaps a mental handicap. He appears retarded. If that boy is able to throw a stone I will pay one hundred dollars, I examined him, I don't think he can throw a pencil. He can't express himself, something was not normal. We have had boys beaten who were six or seven years old and they speak very well. Oh, we have such pity."

It was the distressed physician who then told us how the soldiers had searched the maternity section of the clinic. In the courtyard outside, where women and their children were waiting to be seen, there was a plaque in English to honor Miss Alice Lalande who was killed when on duty in the same plane that took the lives of the former Secretary-General Dag Hammarskjold and others in the service of the United Nations. Someone kept the plaque clean. But the image of the mute whipped child made it too hard to remember what cease-fire in 1961 the doomed man hoped to bring about, exactly where in Africa.

The boy was never traced, he had been sent to a Red Cross office but was not known there so it was thought that someone on the street knew his identity and led him home.

There was no way to trace him but the entry of armed men into the delivery room demanded an inquiry, useless as it was. The Israeli Defense Forces accommodate reporters who have questions about the actions of soldiers but there is never a face-to-face meeting with an officer unless the circumstances are exceptional. The procedure was to call the public information office in Jerusalem and request an explanation of a specific incident. When this was done an Israeli officer called the hotel in Gaza to say, in English, that "during the chase" local security forces "who had waited a long time captured the man." But no one was captured, only a sleepy night watchman outside was seized.

Language became a mockery when the army used its official voice, the intent always to obscure not clarify. But the Gazans, with their tragic sense of life, used language as a crucial instrument, a consolation, for they had little else and needed its power. Some people were reminded of the Irish when Palestinians spoke. Yet the women in Gaza always put things more plainly than men, in a blunter and stubborn way, without their bardic tendencies. They were not oracular. Very often the woman might say, in an account of some calamity, that she had fallen into shock or knew terror but men gave richer recitals, weaving black and shiny lace into their speech as if they alone saw the wider world. So it was not unusual that a schoolmaster, whose son had just been arrested, hearing me tell how different it was to be back in Gaza after a visit to the West Bank, said: "Those whose hand is inside the fire are apart from the man whose hand is in water."

More and more women were feeling the fire. At twenty-nine Naela Zaquot was admired not just for twice being imprisoned but for having her infant with her the second time so the baby's first months of life were in a cell. Her husband Jamal was once more in jail, then taken out to be deported in 1988 to Lebanon so he did not know their son and had never held him. Deportation by the Israelis was an extreme punishment which caused such international disapproval that Graham Greene and John le Carré had sent a letter to newspapers condemning it. The little boy, Majd, who was one year old that February, made other Palestinians smile and fuss over him for he had been the youngest political prisoner in their history. There had been enormous publicity about this woman named Naela Ayesh Zaquot and the infant, provoking protests from many places and a petition with a thousand names, demanding their release. Her sentence was shortened to four and a half months from six.

"This child is not like other children," Naela said in the spring, recalling how after they were freed the year before, in October, the boy could not easily tolerate a closed door or having the door shut when he was inside a room. Now, playing by himself in the garden at Marna House, he seemed a normal child of fifteen months, and women kept telling the mother this—we all did—so she would not worry.

The stoic woman did not prosper from all the praise for her courage. The political principles, the allegiance to Palestine, were already dipped in steel. What was draining her was the constant longing for her husband. In those months she did not know where he lived and could not telephone. And she was still not safe and wished to be although too proud to make such an admission. Lonely and sad she was grateful for her job as a project coordinator at the Save the Children office in Gaza. While in prison with the boy, the organization had continued to pay her salary. In the office on Omar Mukhtar Street, in a handsome old villa behind a wall, she looked like any working woman, in pretty Western clothes with the big shoulders and loose jackets that were in fashion everywhere. She never covered her head, and her hair might have been cut short in Paris or New York. She was the new Palestinian woman, some people said, but only Naela knew what price had been paid. Her mother kept hoping she might gain some weight.

"The women in the intifada can do anything, almost the impossible," Naela said. "In the light of harsh, traditional social customs they are always limited so it was difficult for us to break the chains. Not an easy task."

In the large apartment where she lived with the parents of her husband, all their faces gave warning it was not the safe and peaceful place it appeared to be. The army came and went and came back. Her husband wrote constantly to relieve his own pain. His letters were read and re-read and almost memorized, a pile of them in a cupboard in the room where Naela and Majd slept. The child had a yellow toy telephone. The father longed for the two of them and the early letters of the banished man shone with misery and longing. He numbered them so she knew five were missing. "I can't tell you how much I want to hold my child. Many times I have seen him in my dreams. The last time Majd was so big and could speak but he wouldn't come to me. Does he know me? Give him my picture so he will recognize me and teach him that I am his father." It was Naela who translated parts of the letter into English, sitting on the big bed. He wrote: "You don't know my sorrow because I am so far from you and my son and my family and my land. Always I keep trying to write you but I don't want to tell you my problems. I live alone in a house. It is terrible . . . and I don't know anybody. It is not comforting. . . ."

She kept showing the boy a photograph of the man—it was a fine, intelligent face—but Majd only looked for a second and could not say the word for father.

In June when Naela and the child were visiting her parents in Ramallah, a city on the West Bank, the soldiers appeared again. The elderly parents were aroused at eleven-thirty P.M. The Israelis banged around the apartment in their usual way, always shouting as if the parents needed a stronger dose of fear. Even on normal days both of them looked glazed with sadness, one son already in the grave, another deported, then the daughter-in-law and their grandson put in jail. The neighbors heard the bedlam and everyone had another night of torn sleep. "Where is the bitch, who does she go around screwing in Ramallah?" one Israeli hollered. The mother had never heard language like this and the father was no less horrified. In Naela's bedroom the soldiers knew what to do, it was easy enough to find the letters of Jamal Zaquot, her own diary—with its record of loss and longing—and that large envelope bulging with press clippings about her imprisonment. They took all of it. She tried not to mind but could hardly bear being robbed of so much. Nothing promised to get better: Naela was not permitted to go abroad and the hus-

band could not come back. He was not able to telephone
and letters had to be sent to Bulgaria where a friend
mailed them to her.

By 1989 she did not much resemble the plumper
girl with the radiant smile, the high-minded diligent
student who had gone to Bulgaria at the age of twenty
to study at the Higher Institute for Medicine to be a
laboratory technician. Palestinians were given privileged
status by the Communist government and there was a
large community of them. Jamal, who had been there
for three years preparing for medical school, was one of
the Palestinians who met her flight, a welcoming committee. It was hardly an impetuous courtship, they were
not given to frivolous attachments, and did not permit
themselves the fast flirtation.

"There were certain shared views, a tremendous
compatibility," said Naela. "He was very kind, an excellent student. For three years there were no love discussions between us." Jamal's life was a graph of torment:
a brother had been deported to southern Lebanon in
1975 and then shot to death in 1978. It was a political
murder, not the killing of a combatant, for the brother
was a member of the Democratic Front for the Liberation of Palestine, and was guilty only of having ideas and
sharing them. And her husband had been in solitary
confinement in Gaza jail before going to Bulgaria.

"The brother was so important to him and it affected my husband so deeply. Poor family," Naela said.
"The father used to be a gardener at UNRWA."

When they were together in Sofia, the devoted students, he must have tried to tell her that there might be
hardships ahead but, so happy in his presence, she was

not able to imagine what her own lot would be. He was so much wiser but the young man could not have foreseen that his wife would suffer as men did by being imprisoned.

It was Jamal who came back to Gaza alone while she stayed on to complete her studies. His next arrest was in 1985, after eight months he was released in April of 1986. Three months later she returned to Gaza and so much later remembered the wondrous reunion and their joy. In December they were married at home and then held a reception at the Love Boat for five hundred people from Gaza and the West Bank, one of the last huge happy celebrations that Gazans so relished before the intifada, a year later, put an end to all that.

Disaster was hissing just behind them and they were too happy to hear, and felt themselves protected. They had been married for two months when they were severed from each other. It happened on a normal evening, after supper, when the family was watching television. The soldiers plunged in like men on a combat assault as if armed Palestinians were waiting in every room. This time there were two Shin Bet women just for her.

"Not a word from any of them but they created a situation of chaos. My father-in-law was led to the kitchen and the door closed. My mother-in-law was put in a bedroom. They took my husband outside where they began to beat him." She was ordered to give up her ID card and get dressed while the women kept guard.

The father-in-law, distraught, opened the kitchen door so many times a soldier started to choke him.

Downstairs, outside the apartment house, were three military vehicles and soldiers ringing the building.

There were two cars of Shin Bet. She wanted to tell one
of the women among her captors that she was pregnant
but was told she was not allowed to speak. That night,
in the police station at Ashkelon in Israel, she was made
to sleep on the floor, her head near the toilet.

The next day the prisoner was taken to Maskubia,
the Arab name for the Russian Compound, property in
Jerusalem once owned by the Russians and converted
into a prison by the Jews. Here the interrogations took
place in a room that was freezing cold because of the
air-conditioning which Gazans did not have. The prisoners always dreaded that, it made their bones shrivel. She
was hooded. Someone accused her of being a member
of the Democratic Front for the Liberation of Palestine
when she was in Bulgaria in 1983.

"There is nothing to tell. What should I tell?
Should I lie, do you want me to lie?" Naela said.

"Yes. Okay, we do, we want a lie from you." The
Shin Bet were taunting her.

On the night of February 24, she began to hemorrhage and called out that she must be taken to the toilet.
The cramps were so severe that she could not easily
stand but was ready to crawl if no one would help her.
Permission was denied.

"You must talk if you want a doctor," said the
guard. Even in pain, she was astonished to hear this.
Later, a man was brought in the cell with an interpreter
but she did not know if he was a doctor or Shin Bet,
someone who might have orders to mutilate or harm
her. He spoke neither Hebrew nor Arabic. There was no
reason to trust him so she refused to be examined or
permit him to come close. Others came, saying an urine

analysis was needed and she filled a cup with dark red
liquid.

By the first of March when the Israeli human rights
lawyer Leah Tsemel was permitted to see her, Naela
believed that her own family would not recognize her so
changed was her face. Another Israeli lawyer, Felicia
Langer—the two women were both loved and reviled
for their efforts to help Palestinian prisoners—called a
press conference to describe Naela Zaquot's ordeal. The
two Jewish women, the furies, worked ceaselessly for by
now the prisoner was nauseous, weak and dizzy. The
lawyers together went to court to appeal for her release
and to file a complaint against Shin Bet.

The ailing woman was allowed to enter a hospital
but only to remain there for three hours with no visitors.
The doctor, an Arab, was kind and proficient but she did
not know exactly what had been done for the term
dilation and curettage, a standard surgical procedure
after miscarriage, was unknown to her. She remembered
blood transfusions and being told her blood pressure was
extremely low.

It was easier for her to speak of this to another
woman and needing privacy we sat in the closed sun
room of Marna House where the ironing was done. In
that large light room where Alya stored a long dining
room table and chairs used in the old days for banquets
Naela went over and over all that had happened. Sometimes her English was not clear, or her voice too low, so
she would have to repeat and repeat, often faltering.
During the miscarriage she had lain in clotted blood and
said aloud her husband's name.

They saw each other in military court but all he

could do was embrace her, whisper, plead: "You must be strong." Others recalled the husband as being obsessed with winning her release. After thirty-five days because of the indefatigable lawyers she was freed, on the grounds of psychiatric suffering, with a fine equaling two hundred dollars and another for the probation period. "The judge appeared—human," Naela said. Any semblance of decency, let alone kindness, seemed remarkable to her.

Together, they came back to life but did not count the days that were left or suspect they were numbered. She began her first job at Save the Children. Their child, named Majd, was born in a hospital in Jerusalem on February 22, 1988, six days after Jamal Zaquot was again arrested and held in Gaza jail. There was no warning that he would be deported and when it happened the family, who had seen him during visits, could not believe it. Journalists told them the news, how Jamal had been taken out and, with six other men from the West Bank, driven to southern Lebanon and dumped. The International Red Cross usually had its own people there to help the men who were without clothes, possessions or money.

"On August first he was gone," Naela said. What she had left was the baby and her job, work that she needed.

When they came back for her—at least thirty-five soldiers with the Shin Bet policewoman—it was a more orderly and formal arrest. No reason was given. A Palestinian was not entitled to due process. This time she was sent to Telmond Woman's Prison in Israel, not knowing the charges, an administrative detainee. In a week her mother-in-law brought the baby to see her.

"He started to laugh when he saw me. 'Let me hold him,' I said to the woman guard. 'It's forbidden to do that,' she said. The baby starts to sob, I cry, and other prisoners begin to weep so the visit transforms itself into a tragedy. I told my mother-in-law: 'Go away, I don't want my son to see me crying.' "

A new Israeli law did permit the separation of mother and child provided the child was two years of age, which Majd was not. A new campaign once again led by Leah Tsemel and Tamar Peleg, the Red Cross and political groups including Women for Political Prisoners, based in Tel Aviv, became so vociferous that the baby was allowed to join his mother in October after an appeal was filed in court. There was international press coverage.

The two of them, once reunited, had a cell to themselves with a toilet and a sink, a bed and a crib. The door was not locked during the day. Two hours a day the prisoners were allowed out, ten to eleven A.M. and then from four to five P.M. The other prisoners waited for a sight of the baby and competed to hold and cuddle him.

"The child made them very happy, most of them had children of their own," she said. "All the women loved him. The doors to all our cells were shut at six-thirty P.M., he always laughed when our door was opened again."

There was a kitchen down the hall where she heated his milk in the cold mornings. The sight of the child, being carried by Naela, made the prisoners more hopeful. But he did not like being shut in every evening.

"There was only one window, small with bars, so what could he see?" Naela said.

The family brought her powdered milk and baby food, other help came from the International Red Cross and a message of support from different Israeli groups opposed to the abuses of the occupation. "In prison I could take care of my child so that's why I kept on and on insisting that he must be with me," Naela said.

She was always in conflict with the prison authorities, it was a point of honor. Chris George, the American director of Save the Children, in the West Bank and Gaza, which built schools, sanitation and water systems, and initiated a farm loan program, remembered visiting Naela in Telmond prison. She remained proud, almost disdainful.

"In fact she was talking to us about something that was unfair, or wrong, in the prison when the guard in the room who overheard her corrected what she said," Mr. George said, later. "Naela snapped right back at her, something to the effect that she shouldn't butt in, or that what the guard said was quite wrong."

When the famous prisoner was freed at last the child found liberty confusing.

"He cried and looked at people with fear. He wanted to hold my hand all the time. It took a week, or more, for him to recover. It's strange but he likes men better than women, perhaps it's his need for a father, that feeling. Before my husband was arrested we were planning many things, we dreamed of our lives in Gaza and he was happy before he went to prison."

Once, walking in the streets with Naela carrying the baby, looking for a taxi to go home, we had to pass soldiers on the corner of El Nassar Street. They were lounging, a few even crouched as if tired. Hers was a beautiful face so some of them stared as all soldiers would but no man spoke, or even made a joke. Carrying the boy, she refused to walk faster as if this might be seen as panic. She learned her composure long ago and never let her head or shoulders droop when the troops were close.

At last a taxi stopped and the women in the bulging back seat squeezed together more tightly to make room for her and the child. Two men sat in the front, a proper arrangement.

The job at Save the Children was a blessing and she was at the office by eight when the workday started in Gaza. There were funds given to small projects started by women: the Bedouins who used homemade dyes for the large rugs they wove on the traditional looms and hoped to sell, the women who formed a collective to make their own biscuits, and then yogurt, which they sold to the store owners. The office shut at the customary hour, three P.M. for people did not take a lunch hour. Majd always spent the day at Miss Barbari's well-run cheerful kindergarten at the Palestine Women's Union where his mother picked him up. They were together until the boy went to bed and the curfew reduced visits from friends. She did not have that many because she had not grown up in Gaza. Hers was hardly the life of the raging revolutionary but she was as guilty as everyone else of wanting a Palestine for Palestinians. No other purpose seemed as great: It held people captive and made of them partisans, fanatics, outlaws, chroniclers, revolutionaries, legends, poets, lawyers, exiles, prophets and neurasthenics but not always. She grew braver and accustomed to her despair.

By that summer she looked much better and was gaining weight. She was now able to speak on the telephone to Jamal, who was living in Cairo, at least once a week and this made her smile more easily. Her husband wanted her to join him there but she balked at the idea of leaving Gaza because it required signing a paper for the Israelis that she would not return for three years. To go was to admit defeat and there was no guarantee that she would not be kept in exile for years. And in Cairo there was little chance of a good job. "She doesn't want to be a kitchen-lady," Sobeh said, struggling to make clear the dilemma which was new to him. But Naela knew that she would leave, sooner or later, that she could not go on living this way.

Once we passed a wall brightened by the green, lovely curves and strokes of Arab calligraphy and she made sense of it. Green was the color often used by Hamas, the Islamic fundamentalist movement, which was ardently supporting the intifada when earlier it had long opposed it, and the P.L.O. The message was only stunning if you could not read a word. It called for a general strike although the sole authority to do this was always Unified Leadership. Hamas, which was not part of the P.L.O. or its parliament in exile, the Palestine National Council, was making its own demands on the population to show its power. It called itself the Islamic Resistance Movement and was outlawed.

"As a woman living in Gaza it is impossible for me

to meet with Hamas. The problem is their problem,"
Naela said. "Sometimes I cannot find an excuse for their
behavior, which I don't think is based on a political
ideology. There is room for tolerance. I do not accept
them."

The record of Hamas was clouded: the Islamic fundamentalists had been useful to Israel because of their
long quarrels with the secular supporters of the P.L.O.
In March 1981 the Israeli Military Governor of the
Gaza Strip, Yitzhak Segev, admitted to David Shipler,
the *New York Times* correspondent in Israel, how he
financed the Islamic fundamentalists as a counterweight
to the P.L.O. and the Communists. He was severely
reprimanded for disclosing this. The Israeli government
gave him a budget and he dispensed funds to certain
mosques. Hamas did not then exist in its present form.

It was thought, although no one easily confirmed it,
that one-third of the population of Gaza and the Strip
were Hamas followers but many of its Palestinian opponents insisted the figure was not higher than seventeen
or eighteen percent. Their very existence gave rise to
alarm in the outside world and there were always predic-
tions that a Palestine state, with Hamas seeking supremacy over other diverse and belligerent political factions,
would create another Lebanon. As the intifada
drummed on, some Gazans admitted that Hamas was a
form of purification that lifted them above the dangers
and the daily disorders. It was an answer to misery. By
being stricter Muslims they found a way to renounce the
Israelis, to distance themselves, to find a coherence that
their daily lives could not provide. It steadied them. But
in a conservative and devout society many religious Ga-

zans were suspicious of Hamas, which was founded in February 1988, believing it wanted to destroy the P.L.O.

A well-known Israeli famous for his intellect and unusual efforts on behalf of Palestinians saw the emergence of Hamas as an impediment to Arab aspirations.

"The immediate great danger of Hamas is creating a difference between the Gaza Strip, where it is so much stronger, and the West Bank," said Israel Shahak, the founder and director of the Palestinian Human Rights Campaign, to the American scholar H. Aram Veeser. "Especially because in Gaza the percentage of Christians is so small while in the West Bank there are more communities. You know the real basic difference between Hamas and the P.L.O. is that Hamas objects to an organization to which the Christians will be admitted on terms of equality." For example, George Habash, leader of the P.F.L.P. who was then living in Damascus, would be cast out by Hamas if they prevailed although he leads the second largest faction in the P.L.O.

A chance came to meet a Hamas dignitary but instructions on comportment were very precise. You are not to touch him, you do not shake hands, the intermediary said, knowing the vagaries of foreign behavior. He could not provide his name, his exact role, if any, or answer questions about the strategy of the fundamentalists for the Israelis were now trying to destroy Hamas since it vehemently supported the end of the occupation. In May the Hamas leader, a young quadriplegic, and his entourage had been arrested; some Gazans believed it was in retaliation for the kidnapping of two Israeli soldiers.

Nothing prepared me, not even having read the Koran three times in English. All the study, all the books on Arab history, did not forestall a sense of impending failure. Dressed as sedately as a British nurse in 1914, in a skirt that barely showed the ankles, wrists, neck and hair were also covered in deference to Hamas' requirements for decency. Gazan women were not even permitted to swim with men and few had ever been in the sea.

The Hamas man, in his long robe, was serene and confident, speaking English easily. It was the plump and happy contours of his face that made him special for most Gazans had expressions of strain, some faces promising headaches or the onslaught of small tics. In a population that did not look rested or decently fed, this shrewd and calm man looked imported. We sat at a suitable distance from each other. It was not an interview but an audience that he was granting, possibly at the risk of delaying his dinner. There was the faint smell of food seeping into the hall, a low clatter coming from the kitchen.

The agnostic is often fascinated by those whose convictions can never be challenged. The imam, swami, bishop, rabbi, priest, even a minor vicar, exert a peculiar fascination for those of the "faithless faith," as an American scholar put it, who often struggle to stay apart and accept the loneliness it bestows. The man from Hamas was not inclined to explain whether the Islamic Resistance Movement would ever join the P.L.O., or on what conditions, or whether it was religion that would bring power or the need for power which now made Hamas so active in the intifada. Still, he tried to clarify in the proficient manner of an army officer who must brief the lowest ranks but keep it simple.

The first point was to emphasize the difference between Gaza's Sunni Muslims and the Shiia "which are far away" in case foreigners confused them and thought that other fundamentalist groups, who took hostages in Iran or Lebanon, were connected to Hamas. He did not mention the taking of hostages but had this in mind.

"Power is not a stable item," he said. "The power which is not dependent on religion will not last. We are believing in God, Allah, we believe in Mohammed, the Prophet. We believe that after this life there is a better life. We follow the orders of Allah and Islamic practice throughout history and this can solve the political and social problems. We are not against Jewish, Catholic and Western countries. If they are dangerous we can fight them." There was a digression, a reference to the Roman Empire as if it were a huge ocean liner which sank because of the depravity of its cargo. The intermediary, who once ran a dress shop, looked relieved that there were no interruptions from me.

"Islam is a system of government, it reveals every aspect of governing daily activity. Smoking, drinking, certain television programs like 'Dynasty' . . ." the Hamas man said, sighing as if he could see the thousands of television sets turned on, the multitude of rapt faces. "Our will to choose this program or refuse it, this is a training and if we prohibit, or forbid ourselves, such bad habits, drinking and sexual orientation, our will will retain its power. It will then be easier for us to ask for our rights.

"The only way we can be very effective is by returning to Islam. The second life counts for the life we have now, the labor pains we are now suffering. We should be distant from a contaminated society. . . . As a medical man discovers a new medicine for cancer, I know that we are the medicine. Aimless and uncontrollable are the Americans and Europeans."

Suddenly it seemed certain that the Hamas man was a doctor, probably an obstetrician, used to being obeyed. Then the clouds gathered in the tidy room with its couches and chairs lined up against the walls. The intermediary stared at his old expensive shoes, and was fearful.

"What is the benefit of woman freedom? What is the difference between (a free) woman and an animal practicing sex? To practice sex like animals is that what is wanted?" He pretended not to see that I had begun to twitch. "Women have the full right to be doctors and lawyers, anyway we prefer women doctors in obstetrics, no objection there.

"The most important thing is peace of mind. The loss of peace of mind is terrible. Millions of men practice sex and are deprived. Marilyn Monroe committed suicide and there was Dalida in France. An actress and a singer. So much money and sex are not peace of mind."

For a second there was the temptation to defend Miss Monroe and explain that a wretched childhood and depression, not excessive intercourse, might have led to her death. Dalida, born in Egypt, a minor recording artist in Paris, was not widely known.

He moved on to the subject of murder and criticized the killings of collaborators by the committees in Gaza. In Islam there were rules which made it permissible to kill, the Hamas man said. He ticked off the three categories. If anyone originates a killing he can be killed; the married man who commits adultery if there are four eyewitnesses; those who abandon Islam. Salman Rushdie's name rose like a small wave, then receded.

"Islam will dismiss the occupation. Allah originated the intifada. We will reach the degree that the angels will help us," he said. *Many as the angels be in heaven their intercession will not avail in the least without God's permission for whomsoever He please and approve,* the Koran says. It would have been unwise to show off and recite this for some Arabs think it is a sacrilege for translations to exist of their sacred text, believed to have been dictated to Mohammed, founder of Islam, by Allah through the angel Gabriel. Then, a silence in the living room as if the three of us were conjuring angels. Sometimes in the houses in Gaza there were pictures on the walls from an old calendar or magazine of angels hovering over the figure of Mary who was greatly favored. They were the usual idiotic-looking cherubs.

Perhaps because he saw that his foreign guest was now morose the devout man sought to end the meeting on a triumphant note.

"We *respect* women!" Hamas said, leading me to the kitchen to meet his wife who he said was a teacher. The handsome woman with pink cheeks was standing over the stove, hair covered, stirring and peering into pots, with three of their seven children scampering in the kitchen. Startled by the sight of a stranger, she gave a charming smile and shook hands since I held mine out. Women were permitted this. Here was Hamas' example of the happy, dutiful, devout woman, proof of all that her husband believed and admired, and at last able to put dinner on the table.

The infidel so despised by the fundamentalists, the loyal Communist who was their enemy, sat in the garden of Marna House for the first time. The smallest room, at twenty-five dollars a night, was more than his family lived on every week. He was thirty-eight years old, he said, and for years he had worked as a manual laborer. The poor never looked younger than they were, their teeth and skin and hands told the truth. But his face was not average, it gave him away, the seeker who had found the treasure. He had spent decades reading and hauled himself out of the abyss of other men whose sight was still clouded and uncertain. He wanted it known right away that Communists did not exploit women in Gaza.

"I had a pair of shoes once and I polished them myself," he said. "I did not ask my wife to do it, never did I expect that. I help with dinner, I mop, I air the mattresses. In our society women are treated like slaves, but I treat my wife like an equal.

"She is very sympathetic. She sees us, the members of the party, as truthful. Our relations with our wives are unique. We do not lie or steal. If I am not going to be just in my own household how will I be just in the society? Many small things in life reveal the bigger things."

He wore a clean short-sleeved shirt and trousers whose bottoms were slightly frayed. His hair was thinning so the broad face looked even larger but was not moody or taut. Talking about his childhood was not interesting to him when his mind was on Engels and Marx but a few details were given. No family could have been poorer or more desperate than his, and there were ten children.

"I am born a peasant, a refugee, in the working class so I had fertile soil to become what I am. Perhaps once a month we ate a little meat but not always. For twenty years I always put on shoes that were never new, not even my pants or any of my clothing were new. In 1948 my mother had to ground *zawan* to make our bread because we could not afford flour. This is a small example of how we lived." *Zawan* was the local Arabic word for the bad kernels of wheat or those infested with insects.

"So where should I go? To the upper classes?" This made him smile, the idea was so ludicrous.

The great upheavals in Europe had already begun, the quick revolutions and demands for reforms, the denunciations and admissions of failure and mistaken policies. He was not shaken or his convictions dented. But he understood the compromises that would have to be made to gain a Palestinian state. Later its imperfections would be the problem.

"In order to get liberation we have to hold hands with all sorts of people in different layers of society. A petit bourgeois democracy is not my final goal but now I have no choice, I cannot talk about the democracy of the proletariat. The Palestinian bourgeoisie is also suffering from the occupation so our main task is teaching all the people about the struggle. We have to work hand in hand with the petit bourgeois to go through this cycle. There is an upper class that sometimes benefits by the occupation, and sometimes is harmed by it. This is the class that will try to rule with their capital and we will have to struggle against that."

The week before thirteen people were sentenced to prison for being Communists, he said, that is what they all had to expect. In the garden he drank coffee but did not want a cigarette. He had given up smoking because it was too expensive. It did not please him to once again hear the slogan of Jabalia Camp that the Americans were stronger than the Israelis and the Palestinians were stronger than the Vietnamese.

"Those who say that are not realistic," the Communist said, solemnly. "We are *not* stronger than the Vietnamese." He did not want to encourage people to be theatrical even if it greatly helped them to keep going.

In 1972 he was sent to prison for ten years and bore it, as if all his life was a preparation for this, a necessary thing if a new generation of men would be created who, in a purer world, would lead lives that did not require or permit violence, submission, coercion or the defeat and ruin of others. He did not seem to care that the fraternal order was shrinking in the wider world. He had never seen the cities of Europe and the possibility of it was so dim.

"In prison they fed us better than I was fed at home. I lived those years with all the feelings of any human. Always take into consideration the goal of the prison administration is to destroy us. I was beaten many times and even taken out when nude so the coldest water could be poured over me. And it was winter." There was more he might have told but did not, perhaps wanting to avoid the pity of a stranger or the sympathetic little cluck in the throat.

Told that some foreigners were amazed by the restraint of the Palestinians during the insurrection, that in other countries enraged citizens would have their revenge even if it brought their own death, the man answered as if he had thought of nothing else for a long time. He went slowly so the words would filter properly through the interpreter from Jerusalem.

"The intifada is a result of the failure of armed struggle. Why did the armed struggle fail? Why is the stone thrown instead of the bomb?" He thought the absence of a strong Arab country to encourage and protect the intifada, and its structural bases, was one reason and it was often cited by others. King Hussein of Jordan was hated because in 1970 his army in Jordan killed an estimated three to five thousand P.L.O. guerrillas to win back control of the country; other Arab heads of state were equally distrusted. "Why there are Jews who do more for us than our Arab brothers," a man in Beach Camp once said and others had to agree. Another reason was a lack of arms, the Communist said. But, most important, was the lack of education among people that was crucial.

"As an example, a kid was shot in a clash in Gaza. His friends took him to a doctor who called the Israeli Army. If we are not capable of taking out a bullet what kind of armed struggle would we have?

"Yes, if the people are ready, I will do it but people are not ready. We, as Communists, are not against armed struggle as you might know. But we do not have the area (space), we do not have the weapons and the

Israelis would demolish houses and orchards. But most of all the people are not ready."

He did not hazard a guess when, or if, they would ever be ready, amused at the question which he perhaps found typically American. Gaza was not South Africa or El Salvador and there was no calendar for victory.

"We are in a unique situation—we are totally different from anyone else," he said.

The afternoon was ending but there was something left to say before he began the long walk to his camp. The cheap taxis still cost too much. His three children might have been waiting for him, the wife starting to cook the evening meal and wondering.

"Wherever we are—in a factory, in the house, in the prison—we are always teaching. Life for us is a school," the man said. "Well, it is not yet our final battle."

He spoke like someone who knew he would not be rewarded for so much pain and loyalty, whatever is thought of as success. The faith was enough and would never desert him. There were factions of the P.L.O. who opposed the Communists and no one believed the party would ever pull in large numbers of Palestinians for its beliefs were too anti-Islamic. He persisted. All the Communist could provide was the hallowed vision and the old ideas; he explained that he had nothing else of value to give his people.

There were always precautions to be taken so he asked for my notebook when he realized his address had been noted, the number of the bloc and the name of the refugee camp. Borrowing a pen he scratched out the four words himself in case an Israeli might examine the pages. There was always that danger. His name had been withheld, not even an initial provided or a nom de guerre. But the address could lead to an ambush.

I saw him once more in his camp, a child leaning against his leg, as he stood talking to another man in one of those clotted alleys, barely wide enough for the two of them. There was no sign of recognition between us, a smile or a nod might have put him at risk. The men were only talking in the last hour before curfew before closing themselves in for the night. That he and I had spoken was another secret, one more, for all of Gaza swallowed thousands of secrets every day and kept watch to see who would give them away.

There were a handful of women who knew nothing about the P.L.O. or Israel and did not dream of what was raging outside their walls. They were nuns in the order of Mother Teresa, who call themselves Missionaries of Charity. They had two buildings on a street in Old Gaza; "Home of Peace" said the small sign in English. One house was for twenty damaged children who were so impaired their families could not keep them and the other, across the street, was for fifteen elderly women in various stages of dementia and regression.

The nuns were from India except for Sister Martine from Galway who had already passed nine years in Yemen, Cairo and Gaza with a lovely spell in Rome. That commonplace country face of Ireland suddenly seemed exotic. She let me see the children who could not speak or walk but wished to be held and the withering women in a fugue state, or conversing with invisible antagonists. The nuns, with their endless cleaning and cooking and nursing, could not take time for a cup of tea. When told they lived in the only safe place in Gaza the nuns did not respond to this dangerous turn in a brief conversation. All they volunteered was that people in the neighborhood were kind. It was not their way to ask for anything or to solicit the smallest contribution. "Bring whatever you wish," Sister Martine said. "We don't need anything." They did, of course: the cheap Egg-crate pads from Caldor's to keep the bedridden from getting sores. Sister Martine did not know about such conveniences, how these bubbled plastic sheets could be cut to size and washed. She was using an old rubber tire to elevate a dying palsied child and could no longer get the second one fixed. When the box from Caldor's was at last bestowed in December Sister Martine was surprised by joy and stammered her thanks. Suddenly hers was the only happy face in Gaza all that year and it was startling to see.

V

Monuments and Flags

THE LARGEST MONUMENT OF ALL IN GAZA—THE most expensive, the most ambitious, the most incongruous, and the most hopeful—was the Cultural Center, a short walk from Marna House on the corner of El Nassar Street. The pale gray square building of ribbed concrete with its low, sloping walls, and pavement, made of perfect rows of small, pale stones, loomed up like a dream and no one drew life from it. Not a single Gazan was curious enough to dare try to enter. The watchman said so. Anyway it was closed to the public and had been there for years so no one still gawked or marveled. With its octagonal skylight framed with orange steel, its long angled windows between concrete panels, it was too graceful and pure to be believed. The main rooms were vast marvels: a library with space for sixty thousand books, an auditorium with a stage which could seat eight hundred people and be divided into smaller areas by high sliding doors covered in an orange vinyl textured material that made the acoustics so good. There was a floor made of natural stone from the West Bank, there was a reception area, there was a terrace with a fountain where people could sit with coffee or food from a little cafeteria, there were offices and two storage rooms for books.

There was a staircase with a long curve and a half-landing that needed eighteen men from Gaza to build. At first the master carpenter said: "I can't do it, how can we curve it?" The architect showed him and later said it was perfectly done. When the staircase was completed in stainless steel, the carpenter stared at it and said: "I did this? This?" It made the architect, a man whose nerves were shredded for years, happy to think of that voice, of the pride of the laborers.

"God is in the details, I've always believed that. I didn't want things to shout," said Saad Mohaffel, thinking of Frank Lloyd Wright. The interiors were faintly Islamic although without a single symbol or cliché. Born a Palestinian he had lived in the United Kingdom since the age of two and was now a successful architect in London. The Cultural Center had swallowed almost a decade of his life and he was not yet done. In the basement men were still working on the plumbing or the air-conditioning.

"Palestinians think architecture is decoration, something with frills but it is the function inside which gives beauty," Mr. Mohaffel said.

It had already cost seven million dollars, not a sum easily imagined in a town where in the camps human waste ran through open drainage ditches, where the lumpy roads had potholes every few feet, and where thousands of children needed shoes and much else. The building held its own sadness: it was a place for Palestinians to show what they were painting, how they danced and sang, what the poets were writing and men of great ideas were thinking yet the perfect rooms were void and mocked meaning.

It had been willed by one man who, in 1973, began musing about a building of grandeur where the world would come to Gaza. His own people would be strengthened and inspired by all the building made possible. But Rashad Shawa, the aristocrat and the visionary, died in 1988. For more than half of his life he had kept protesting the damage done to the Palestinians and believed the center would replenish them.

"He wanted to show people they are of value because of their heritage," Mr. Mohaffel said. "He always felt that people should not be cut off from this." Money was raised from the Benevolent Society of Gaza and far richer Arabs and their governments. Alya Shawa, when asked about the empty Cultural Center, never spoke of her uncle or that singular obsession. Occasionally she permitted herself a sigh. Shawas were loyal to each other, living or dead, for the family mattered most to Gazans.

But the name of Rashad Shawa still infuriated many men in Gaza who thought by criticizing the P.L.O. he had indulged in blasphemy. Others admired him and some still resented his hauteur, his money, his orchards, his self-possessed pronouncements. The center was often seen as his place not theirs. In his book, *Prisoners of God,* the English journalist David Smith wrote of this powerful, haunting man who tried to tell everyone how to be. After a frivolous youth spent in Beirut, Cairo and Amman, Mr. Shawa came back to Gaza in 1949 and let his voice be heard by all. "Under the Egyptians he acquired power by acquiescing in their use of the Strip as a springboard for political attacks on Israel. After the 1967 war he flexed that political muscle to make himself indispensable to all parties in the conflict. Appointed Mayor of Gaza by the Israelis in 1972, then deposed in 1981, he kept an open line to King Hussein, his natural ally, and the P.L.O.," Mr. Smith wrote. In 1986 in a broadcast from Amman which was heard throughout the territories Mr. Shawa denounced Yasir Arafat and made the case for new leaders of the P.L.O. who would negotiate with Israel, then a treasonous idea to many in Gaza. There were death threats and plans to assassinate him but he survived all of it. Some of the plots to kill him were serious but blocked by Fatah, who thought Rashad Shawa was too useful to them as a middleman to be done in. In earlier years Mr. Shawa was seen as too pro-British during the Mandate by men in the other ruling Gaza family, the Souranis, although good manners between the clans were always maintained. And his contacts with the Israelis made nationalists like Mousa Sourani, grandfather of Raji, suspicious.

The Cultural Center was meant to be Rashad Shawa's voice speaking in triumphant deep chords: *This is what we are, this is what we will always be.* But for all its beauty, it spoke of another defeat.

Once the architect was chosen, Mr. Shawa never stepped back and let the young man get on with it. He interfered, he meddled, he saw everything, he gave opinions.

"I've never seen anyone so sharp and forceful," said Mr. Mohaffel. "He was very sophisticated. He wanted to see every detail from something electrical or mechanical to the plumbing."

The building rose in groans. A long series of unenvisaged hostilities from the Israelis delayed the work and raised the cost. The Israeli contractors hired to lay the foundation did a calamitous job in pouring the concrete to the shock of the architect, who imagined their work and professional ethics would be equal to that of Europeans. Then there was the constant "underhanded harassment" from the Israeli authorities, the architect said. They would let materials stay at the docks for six months and would double customs duties. None of this was foreseen by the elderly autocratic Gazan although he should have been less trusting.

"Their approach is very negative. Mr. Shawa wanted the center to be *out* of politics," said Mr. Mohaffel. He did not know that in Gaza nothing ever is. A less persistent man might have wept and stayed in London but the architect was pulled back by love for his creation.

Over the years contractors and subcontractors, carpenters, masons, tile layers, bricklayers, electricians, plumbers, mechanical engineers, and landscape designers came, worked, and went. Andrew Walker, a thirty-eight-year-old plumbing contractor from London, first came to Gaza to work at the Cultural Center in March 1982. He returned in June of 1982, then again in September and November, in March of 1983, back in May, then June and September of 1987, staying for six to eight weeks at a stretch. He saw that the Palestinian laborers, who were good workers, did not want to finish too quickly for jobs were so scarce. He did not harangue them, he knew how poor men managed any way they could. Andrew Walker looked like a football player with his wide chest and massive legs although he was not tall. He wore T-shirts and shorts every day and his manner was polite and unhurried. The BBC crowd making their documentary at first bemused him, he had never met journalists. When the occasional Englishman arrived, a journalist or expert on the Arab world with lovely diction and expensive shirts, Mr. Walker did not say much at dinner as if they each came from a different country. It often touched him that the small crew of Gazans in the center who worked full-time were so eager and intelligent and he liked their company.

"Abed now is very quick to learn, I showed him to caulk a lead joint in cast iron and he twigged it pretty quickly," Mr. Walker said that spring. "Now we are putting in chemicals into the air-conditioning and heating system and Abdullah learned the names of all the chemicals. They ask 'what's that? what is it for?' They're proud of what they have achieved but they can't see who it benefits." In the early years the Palestinians invited him home for dinner or tea, without the slightest self-consciousness or shame that they were so much poorer. He might have enjoyed a beer with them but it was forbidden for the others to drink. There was a new protocol to learn.

"The husbands went in and got the food. What you would get is only a fleeting glimpse of the wife. The rules are: don't look at women, don't whistle at women, don't shake hands, don't ever touch. They are a very hospitable people, a very pleasant people, very engaging. They'd give you the last pound in their pocket." Sometimes he would play soccer with about twenty Gazans in a playground before the intifada but Andrew Walker would always tell you how bad it was even before the uprising began.

It jolted the Englishman to see how the Palestinians were treated although he was not a man who had led a sheltered cushy life. It was the arrogance of the Israelis, Mr. Walker always said, that was hard to bear.

The first year he and a Palestinian were working on the roof of the center which overlooked the headquarters of the Civil Administration when there were many fewer buildings and more open space. He watched as two soldiers pulled in a man from the street and inspected his ID card. The Arab was made to stand with his face pressed against the wall while keeping his arms straight out on either side. If he dropped his arms the two soldiers began to use their rifle butts on him, or kicked him between the legs. "It was in the afternoon, in May 1982. Seeing this I threw a wobbly," said Mr. Walker, who fancied his English slang. "I started shouting at them from on top of the building 'Leave him alone, you fucking wicked bastards!' " A Palestinian forced him to stop and made him get off the roof.

His memories of Rashad Shawa were not joyful.

"He was a tyrant who ruled with an iron fist. Oh, very aristocratic, no time for his workers even if he spent most of his adult life, since 1948, trying to improve the condition of the Palestinians," the plumber said. "He was a modern day Fagin, the wages paid on site were less than the wages paid by other contractors in Gaza."

He stayed clear of the Israeli soldiers, knowing his temper might get him into trouble, but always remembered the day when three high-ranking officers visited the site.

"They asked me what I was earning and I walked away. An Irishman working with us said to them: 'None of your business.' " Andrew Walker could not easily put up with men who governed others, the snobs and the bullies, or the sight of the fist coming down on the helpless man, as if his own life had taught him something about the crueller uses of power and privilege. The Palestinians, who at first had trouble understanding his thick glottal speech, liked him because he was without airs and did not condescend. He did not think of himself as their superior. A patient and careful teacher on the site, he understood how their lives were deformed, how men can drown if always forced to swallow their pride.

"The Israelis got no respect for the Palestinians, they don't treat them as men, they treat them as mud," he said, shaking his head.

He had been coming back to Marna House for so many years that he remembered when the little hotel was run by Mrs. Hilda Jackson, the daughter of the original owner Margaret Nassar, who died in 1982. Some Gazans still called Marna House Mrs. Nassar's place. Mrs. Jackson, who was married to a Scot, reminded the Englishman of a middle-class woman in his own country with her ladylike dresses, the many cups of tea, a matron with a strict code of conduct. He had fun in those first years, going to the Love Boat at night, or to restaurants, making new friends, working the long hours. He rather liked being in Gaza for short spells and one year even came back to Marna House with his wife, and two small sons, which pleased Alya Shawa.

In England, he had once thought of all Palestinians as terrorists or lunatics but now he saw them as an honorable, and decent, people.

"I can leave my room open, the wallet out, and it won't be touched. I can leave my watch and ring on the dresser. Nothing has ever been touched," he said.

He never complained at being hemmed-in that spring when every night meant dinner at Marna House, and the long evenings in the garden. If there was a daytime curfew he went to work anyway even if the

Palestinians could not show. He did his own laundry in his room and when the cook could not come to work because of curfew, Andrew Walker made breakfast for everyone. At night he would sometimes talk about the old days in Gaza, what a vibrant place it had been, and shared the odd scraps of history that he kept hoarding.

"The rats are gone. In 1982 and 1983 Israelis put out poison. In 1983 Gaza was overrun with rats. The number of cats has really gone up," said Mr. Walker. Down the street masked boys were writing their intifada slogans on the walls while, in the dark, friends kept watch. The same wild cats stalked the garden of Marna House and found no solace.

Apparatus needed for the pipes at the center had not arrived and he could not wait for it any longer. Mr. Walker thought he would be coming back again—it would be his tenth trip—but when the Cultural Center was at last finished he was not certain why any Gazans would rejoice.

Other dead men had their monuments too in the cemetery of Gaza, a hilly place overrun by an army of huge, greedy cacti that always grew so happily in the Strip and, here, cut off the dead with their high, bristling barriers. There were small, crooked paths where the cacti had been forced back so that the people might walk without injury. The watchman led the way to the most conspicuous and loved shrine, down an incline to a low clearance where three men lay together. A little roof of corrugated tin protected the raised cement tombs whose tablets paid honor in short clear citations below inscriptions from the Koran.

They were not meant to be the ornate or pretentious graves of the rich who were put in family plots. But the little group, lined in a row on a cement floor so the earth could not disturb them, held greater importance than all other graves. The deaths of the three men were buried inside the lives of thousands of other men. The most famous of the slain men, all young, all remembered for a wild bravery, a noble delirium, was Muhammed El-Aswad. He was known everywhere by another name which he chose. It was in honor of a Cuban Marxist revolutionary who was also a doctor, an economist, a military theoretician, a banker and a veteran of the Cuban revolution who died in Bolivia trying to open a second front in Latin America to help Vietnam during its war with the United States. One Vietnam, two Vietnams, three Vietnams. It was not a name that many students in American universities still knew but in Gaza it was another matter although by now the Cuban's life was dimming among the younger men.

The tablet on the first grave read: "Muhammed El-Aswad. He was known as Gaza's Che Guevara Leader of the Popular Front Forces in Gaza. Killed by Israeli Soldiers March 9, 1973." The tablets were not uniform: for Kamel Hanon and Abed El-Hadi, killed on the same day, there was a sentence saying each had spent his life serving God and statehood.

After 1967 because the Arab world had now lost all of Palestine armed struggle in Gaza was not a choice but an honorable imperative. Che Guevara rose to be the commander of the feyadeen of the P.F.L.P, whose military actions accounted for nearly seventy percent of the armed resistance in Gaza and the Strip. So many years later men who had never known him would tell stories

and more than one was certain that the Israeli general
and politician Moshe Dayan had once said: "We run
Gaza by day but at night it belongs to him." Troublesome Gaza, with its street warfare and guerrilla operations, made Dayan decide to send in another general,
Ariel Sharon, to pacify the area once and for all.

Those who knew the hunted man were certain Che
Guevara would be killed and even Dr. Habash asked him
to leave Gaza. He refused. Rashad Shawa, then the
mayor appointed by the Israelis, proposed to the young
Palestinian that if he would only go abroad the Israelis
would not interfere. But the resistance leader did not
think such an agreement would be honored and it offended him. The house where the revolutionary leader
and three of his officers lived belonged to an uncle of
Raji Sourani, who rented it to a Palestinian doctor because he was living abroad. Unbeknownst to the land-
lord the doctor let the wanted men stay there. When the
Israelis attacked the house at night the Palestinians refused to be captured and opened fire. With the death
of their own Che the Gazans lost heart and seemed to
fall into a long sleep.

In the cemetery, the interpreter did not want to talk
standing at the foot of the graves or translate the lines
from the Koran, which he thought would be blasphe-
mous. The watchman, a silent and stout man, looked for
the thousandth time at the famous graves, and at the
cacti with their fierce claims on the place.

"The dead hear everything but cannot respond,"
Sobeh said as the watchman spoke. "He believes the
souls of the dead hear everything." Circling around the
graves a foot kicked up an old 7-Up can. There was litter

even on the sacred spot, a crushed empty box of cigarettes, a scrap of newspaper. The watchman saw the
foreigner's surprise at the garbage, even here.

"It's the fault of the visitors," he grumbled. "I constantly ask people to pick it up and they don't pay
attention."

Someone had drawn the symbol of the Popular
Front on Che's grave, which was fitting enough. And a
single sentence was lightly written on the side of his
tomb: "Your blood enriches our revolution." There was
an outline of the map of old Palestine on the second
grave and on the third grave the sentence: "Your blood
is the light of our revolution." There were little slots for
photographs of two of the dead men but they were
empty. Soldiers once came to find the grave of Che
Guevara Gaza and broke the tablet which had been
repaired.

Some Gazans hurled their deaths at the Israelis as
soldiers might use hand grenades, as if each dead man
would reclaim a mile of their stolen land, as if each
corpse would lift the others that much closer to victory.
It was not just an Arab reverie, the self-induced pathos
of a people at the end of their rope. In different countries that Palestinians could hardly imagine other men
had used their deaths to prevail.

Listening to the talk of this man's death or that
one's death, never described as defeat, was to hear again
the boy drummers marching in an IRA funeral twenty
years ago in Belfast. All that Palestinians kept saying had
already been sung out in two sentences by an Irishman
in 1920 in his inaugural address when he became the
Lord Mayor of Cork. It was Terence MacSwiney, a poet

and an officer commanding an IRA brigade, who said: ". . . the contest of our side is not one of rivalry or vengeance, but of endurance. It is not those who can inflict the most, but those who can suffer the most who will conquer." Sixty-one years later MacSwiney's words marked the monument for one of the ten IRA men who starved themselves to death in Long Kesh prison in the hunger strike of 1981.

Many men in Gaza knew the name of Bobby Sands, the first to die in the hunger strike, and long ago understood the meaning of MacSwiney's words. "Heaven has a red-colored gate that can only be opened with bloody hands," a Palestinian said, whose two sons were in prison. Some sympathetic Westerners grew impatient with this capacity for suffering and wondered why the Gazans didn't go on a hunger strike, ten thousand of them, to force the Israelis to peace talks with the P.L.O., why they didn't take drastic action. But the orders to do this did not come from Chairman Arafat in Tunis.

Each story of suffering rose like a little monument that the enemy could never see. In this way the Gazans gave evidence and paid homage using their voices as marble, granite and stone. In the prisons men wrote poems and novels but no one was keeping a journal of daily life in Gaza. It might be found when the soldiers searched yet dozens swore it would all be remembered and with each rising of the moon the Gazans would someday speak of their heroes, and their losses.

In the spring evenings the forty-one-year-old surgeon Dr. Ahmed Yasgi could be seen going home after a long day at Shifa Hospital; he lived across the street from Marna House. It was easy enough to get to the apartment even after the curfew fell. He was accustomed to speaking to foreigners and spoke rapidly in his agitation.

"Americans from all directions," said Dr. Yasgi of the foreign delegations who had visited Gaza. He gave the usual introduction to the story he needed to tell, Palestinians are not blunt and direct, they must first begin with a small, mournful, proud aria.

"We are speaking of facts," he said. "If they are going to punish us they have enough reasons. There is no need to be afraid, we'll never be afraid, we are all part of our nation, tens of thousands have gone to jail, had gunshot wounds, people of all ages have been beaten, assaulted inside their homes. . . . It is our destiny."

In Shifa Hospital, two blocks away, there had been pandemonium the day of the accident, December 9, 1987, when it was thought the truck driver meant to kill the Palestinians. I.D.F. troops stormed the hospital, as if it were a citadel and the day was theirs. Shifa was crowded with the injured, their families, friends and neighbors. He could only use his eyes to summon the horror he wanted so much to describe: the madhouse his hospital had become, a scene of slaughter.

"The army was beating patients in front of the doctors and assaulting the medical teams. I saw a patient being knocked down and said: 'Oh, stop—stop.' The soldiers punched me on the shoulder in front of two little girls. Ten times we were trying to protect the staff but the army didn't respect anyone. And a man was killed inside the hospital on December fifteenth. Yes, Ibrahim El-Sakhla. He came with his wife who was one month pregnant."

He thought that fifty to one hundred soldiers were inside the hospital that day, on a sweep for suspects, or anyone whose face annoyed them. Young men were being stalked. The sight of rampaging soldiers enraged one Gazan man with his wife, pushed him into a moment of white fury, so that he made a reckless last stand. The man opened his shirt and faced a soldier less than thirty-two feet away, as if the two of them were alone on a stage, and it was he who must speak first. "If you want to kill anyone then kill me!" the Palestinian shouted. Fifteen people were watching. The soldier knew how to answer and fired. Ibrahim Sakhla lurched into the arms of Dr. Yasgi, needing to speak. He said something about his wife and began his death.

The first faint outline of a monument was now rising and there was another name to be put on it. It was Raid Shihata, an eighteen-year-old boy from Beach Camp who that same month came to give blood for donations that were urgently needed. By then hundreds of boys, in shifts, were trying to defend the hospital by throwing stones and rocks at the soldiers outside. The barrage was often heavy. But Raid was only looking for the blood bank when he was sighted.

"I remember him well. I was standing in front of the surgical hospital when we heard gunshots—the army was trying to invade again. An Israeli aimed for his mouth and he was filled with blood. We carried him to the operating room to do a tracheotomy. There was severe bleeding and a neurosurgeon was needed. He died fifteen days later." But not where he would have wished for all critical cases were sent to hospitals in Israel.

In the street the ambulances wailed. The gate at

Marna House was shut for the night. That day a girl had been shot in the neck and Dr. Yasgi talked about the effects of the different bullets the Israelis used, and one bullet in particular which he thought resembled a modified dumdum which expands greatly inside the body. It scattered shrapnel everywhere and the tiny pieces were difficult to remove because there were far too many of them. He could go on for quite some time about all the bullets—all the surgeons could—and the different wounds made in the eye, the nasal cavity, the skull, the spinal cord, chest, legs and stomach. Once tear gas came into the operating room when he was delivering a baby and he feared the infant might die the fumes were so lethal. And he had never seen so many fractures, compound and multiple, as among his beaten patients.

He was thinking of a six-year-old boy from the Domosh family who had been prancing around, making the V-sign at the Israelis. The soldiers then made sure that his arm would never work as well again. By now it was an old story: the children never expected that armed men would carry out such deliberate revenge.

"I was astonished by the severity of the fracture of the elbow. They chased him and made the boy lie down and jumped on his right arm," the physician said.

He always tried to keep his face free of sadness or any strong expressions. It was critical that he not show his own torment.

"It is very difficult for me to weep because the nurses behave according to my face and junior colleagues too," Dr. Yasgi said. That year it was quieter in Shifa Hospital but no one thought of it as a sanctuary. Sometimes, after a busy day in Gaza, when it was rumored the army was coming in, the male patients would lie awake in their beds listening for those footfalls with the faces of condemned men.

In the early fierce months of the intifada the boys of Gaza did their best to protect the people inside the hospital and many others tried to help. The surgeon remembered a man, who looked ninety years old, handing stones and rocks to those on the front line. He collected them in a sack for the next assault. He stood just behind the boys keeping them supplied, he was not too frail to do that.

After twelve years on the staff as a general surgeon, Dr. Yasgi was dismissed on June 18, 1989. He appeared before the Israeli civilian named David Cohen who was chief of government employees. The surgeon defended himself vigorously and need not have bothered. At first he did not understand that his work was hardly the issue.

"Most of the time I was speaking to myself, explaining that I didn't manage any patient wrongly, that I never came late. He told me that he received a letter from the authorities making two points," the tired man said. "He said: 'You are a leader of El Fatah in Gaza and you are in touch with P.L.O. leaders in Amman.'"

It was a typical accusation: the man was never simply a member of Fatah, he was always the head. His appearance still showed the shock he felt for Dr. Yasgi now looked drained and less certain in his bearing. He wanted to repeat all that he had said to the imperturbable Mr. Cohen.

"How am I, working as a surgeon, able to be leader of Fatah? There are more than forty thousand men in jail who belong to Fatah. If any of the forty thousand say that I am their leader then okay. How can I be the leader when none of them know me? How can you throw me out in the street before you make an investigation or even arrest me?"

It was true that he often spoke to peace groups in Israel, and the delegations, and that what he said was sometimes printed in newspapers. He had seen too much to hold his tongue but perhaps believed a surgeon would be safe from retaliation. Although entitled to two months of severance pay he received nothing and the pension was gone too. It was a hard blow for a man with a wife and two small children and whenever he talked of Shifa he still called it "our hospital" forgetting his dismissal. Conditions were wretched there.

"In our hospital the number of all employees—doctors, nurses, orderlies—was less than two to every bed. In some Israeli hospitals there are five, and one nurse to every forty patients. Sometimes during the night there are only one or two nurses for a whole ward. There are forty beds for female surgery, sixty-five to seventy for male surgery, seventy to eighty beds for gynecology and obstetrics.

"The food is very bad, the worse type and the way of giving it to the patients is inhuman. Throw it at them like that! The kitchen doesn't observe medical precautions and they serve the same food to the diabetic, the heart disease patient. The place is dirty because of the seventy people employed to clean it—the workers—they are using forty of them for other jobs.

"An ambulance takes two hours to pick up a patient. There are fourteen ambulances without equipment, just passenger car ambulances, no oxygen. The shortages!

And such measures to prevent infection—we sent patients home immediately. For exploration I only keep them two days, after an operation where there are stitches I send them home in five days. Well, many patients refuse to stay because they are afraid."

It was his tendency to use the present tense in English although he was fluent.

"At the beginning of the intifada the army asked people to pay but they refused because they were injured by the army. The rates"—he gave a little snort—"are one hundred twenty dollars a night. People who have health insurance pay four hundred dollars a year for it, more or less. All the doctors are paid the same, no difference between specialist and general surgeon. It's six hundred dollars a month."

In the cases of wounded refugees, the hospital bills were covered by UNRWA.

After being notified of his dismissal Dr. Yasgi tried to see that the junior doctors were advised on the condition of his patients. Then he saw his life spinning away.

"I was very active, jumping from place to place. I have passed more than twenty years as a doctor. Now I feel very old and tired. Anything can affect me. I feel a lot of depression and when I hear of anything Jewish I become severely nervous.

"Oh, I am not looking for money. The patients are as dear to me as my sons and my wife. I used to be the giver. Now I cannot tolerate the news that ten persons are injured when I cannot help. I feel severe depression, it's incredible."

It was said that he came from a wealthy family, that relatives owned and ran the 7-Up plant, but that was of little consolation to the surgeon who wanted to go on with his own work. If you spoke his name at Shifa Hospital, months after his dismissal, the male nurses only answered with sad, shut faces. It was too dangerous to speak, the prominent surgeon was an example of what could happen to anyone. But they pretended not to notice if a foreigner wanted to move around the wards, asking the old questions about bullets and soldiers, time and place please.

The dead and the missing came back at night, talking to us in their normal voices, as the documentaries were watched at Marna House after dinner. There was the handsome old face of Rashad Shawa, in an Irish film, and his low monarchical voice saying that Palestinians might prefer death to their lives of degradation. And there was the twenty-four-year-old male nurse, Abed Ajrami, in the wards of Ahli Arab Hospital with the wounded children and then, sitting at home in Jabaliya, talking over the noise of rounds being fired in the camp. He had been arrested on November 26, a Sunday, and as we watched him in the BBC documentary, *Life Under Occupation,* he had already undergone interrogation by the Shin Bet in Gaza Central jail. It was jarring to once more see that thin, remarkable twenty-four-year-old man with the deep-set eyes and high, radiant smile. "The more suffering we have the more hope we have. . . . History teaches us that no occupation lasts forever," Abed said, the camera on his long, intelligent face. Now he had been hooded beaten kicked and shackled.

Coming back to Gaza that December for the last time, I dreaded hearing which man had been taken and where, and for what reason. The reasons were often unknown. Once in the summer, on his day off, Abed took me to Jabaliya Camp to see his house, as crowded as any of them, stopping at a demolished structure whose walls looked like the stumps of huge broken teeth. A couple was haunting the place, it once had been theirs. There was still a sink and a corner that had not crumbled but the roof was gone. In a patch of earth, where a flood had once been, there was a minuscule garden, between chunks of fallen walls. We stared at the two green stalks pushing to the sun and the man who had lived there bent to pat the soil on one side. It was his new garden.

"This is what I love and admire so much in the people," said Abed. Perhaps he went to jail because of us, the foreigners so eager to learn and then to leave. Some Gazans thought it was because of the BBC film but the documentary had been cleared by the Israeli censor and aired months before his arrest. But everything put him in danger, each meeting with a foreigner, and there were spies in that No Man's Land with communiqués to deliver.

In the main room of his house, where a small bed was the couch, there was a poster of a pale, insipid-looking little girl with a huge basket of flowers which he thought was peaceful and pretty. And there was a photograph from a magazine of a fine large brown horse on another wall, without a saddle or bit. The television set was covered with a blue and white cloth during the day and 7-Up stickers were decoration for an armoire. On the front door were the red letters from an old issue of the cover of *Time* so anyone could find the place.

Abed did not know the pleasure people felt in his

presence. It was not just the appealing appearance but more the generous spirit, the surprising gentleness in a perverse and cruel place. Love took visible form when he was working with his patients. But he was not a large or bulky man and there was reason to fear that his face, and hands, might enrage his captors who would beat him all the harder to destroy what was so pretty.

People saw his promise and no one more than Dr. Swee Chai Ang, the orthopedic surgeon at Ahli who worked with Abed for six months. After she was not permitted to stay in Gaza and left it was obvious how much Abed missed her. They worked together very well in the wards and in the small orthopedic clinic near the entrance of the hospital compound where he would assist her and translate. A gift seemed in order that summer to cheer him up and he was pleased with the red and white striped shirt I bought but he never wore it. A friend his age saw the new shirt and borrowed it.

"He liked it too much," Abed said, laughing. Gazans were generous and undemanding. No Palestinian ever asked me to bring them anything from the United States except for another male nurse, in the Eye Hospital, who was trying to build up a medical library and longed for a copy of the English textbook, *A Color Atlas of Ophthalmological Diagnosis* by M. A. Bedford, the honorary consulting surgeon at Moorefield Eye Hospital.

"Sometimes I dream of going to Sweden and having the life of any young man but I can't—there is my family and my work," Abed said. He was obliged to be strict with himself, his was the only income for eight people. There were the elderly parents, two older married brothers with children who were both without jobs, and three younger boys. His three sisters were married. No child had done as well as Abed, a graduate of the Baptist School of Nursing at Ahli Arab Hospital, run by Americans, where he was chosen president of the student body. In his entire life he had rarely known a frivolous day. Sometimes the hours at Ahli were so long it was Dr. Swee who had to drive him home in a U.N. vehicle since the curfew had long been in effect. It made people smile to remember that she was so small her head was not much higher than the steering wheel. Often, in the evenings, she would come to Marna House where Alya tried to get her to eat some dinner but unless food was put on her plate she forgot it was there, and began to talk about the new patients. She did not want to sleep or eat. Another English surgeon took her place and then left to go back to Liverpool. There was no surgeon in December for orthopedics so Abed was transferred to the emergency room. He missed the old days and the clinic.

Coming back in winter to that room with the horse and the little girl with flowers, everything always in place, was to find the family assembled, and hear their low dirge. It was twenty-five days before word came where Abed was being held, the mother said and the men in the room did not look at her face as she kept holding up a black and white photograph, a portrait. The father, with the white skull cap and a rough handsome face, had nothing to add as if all human speech was useless. Abed was working the night shift at the emergency room when the soldiers came for him, a summons was left for him to report at nine A.M. the next day to the military. "He said, 'I haven't done anything, so there is nothing to worry about,' " the mother said, twice.

All the men in his family had the same profile as Abed but the older brothers looked worn down, faces grated by years of worry and uncertainty, and now this. Not only Abed was gone but a younger brother had been arrested in October. The room was filled with foreboding, and in her pain the mother could not sit quietly as the men did. The brothers lived next door, the lives of the family were tightly woven together.

The fear was that Abed would be killed during interrogation by the Shin Bet; a man died on December 19 during questioning in Gaza jail but it was many months before it was known that he had been murdered. Although an Israeli military spokesman initially stated that the twenty-seven-year-old Palestinian, Khaled Kamel Sheik Ali, died of a heart attack, the facts were different. On December twenty-fifth, Dr. Michael Baden, co-director of forensic science for the New York State Police, traveled to Israel for the American organization, Physicians for Human Rights, to observe a six-hour autopsy on Khaled Ali. Both Dr. Baden and an Israeli pathologist, Dr. Yehuda Hiss, concurred that "the cause of death was blunt trauma to the abdomen resulting in laceration of the mesenteric plexus and intra-abdominal hemorrhage. The autopsy also revealed deep bruises to the arms and legs and hemorrhage in the testes," a report said in the publication of Physicians for Human Rights. The two pathologists traveled to Gaza where they saw the room where the prisoner died and spent two hours questioning the Shin Bet agents who admitted to having had Khaled Ali as their prisoner. They denied any physical mistreatment of the dead man.

Blunt trauma to the abdomen meant the prisoner was kicked to death.

More than six weeks passed and still the young lawyer in Gaza could not see the prisoner known as Abdel Razik (Abed) Ajrami, Identity Card number 949876296. There were letters for him, one from the three young Englishwomen in London who worked on the BBC film and wanted him to know that he was always in their thoughts and prayers. The lawyer, Sharhabeel Alzaeem, could not even locate his client in the first weeks let alone deliver mail or some of Abed's own clothes. The International Committee of the Red Cross sent one of its representatives to Gaza jail and reported the prisoner had been beaten. A campaign was started to help Abed in London led by his old friend Dr. Swee, who was working with Medical Aid for Palestinians, the private charity which had sent her to Gaza to work in Ahli Arab Hospital and considered Abed under its wing, one of its own. The Ambassador to Israel in the United Kingdom replied himself to an inquiry about Abed from Lord Mishcon, a well-known lawyer, a member of the House of Lords, and a man who was active in Jewish affairs, saying the nurse "was being detained due to his continuing hostile terrorist activity." At that date the lawyer had not yet seen the prisoner and Abed had not appeared before a judge, yet guilt was assumed. Using those very words "hostile terrorist activity" justified any act and always gave legitimacy to lawlessness.

In Jerusalem, Bill Warnock, director of World Vi-

sion, an international Christian relief and development
organization, who was a friend of Abed's, struggled to
make sense of the events and to help. He was able to see
a "confession" signed by Abed which was written in
Hebrew. It was dated November 29, 1989, three days
after the arrest, although the Red Cross was told in
December that Abed was still under investigation and
had not confessed or been charged with any offense.
Such contradictions were commonplace.

It was a peculiar confession, less than seven hundred
and fifty words, taken down by Shlomi Abraham, police
officer. It mentions the names of four other Palestinians
and various transactions that Abed allegedly carried out
and refused.

All confessions were usually suspect since the Shin
Bet told the prisoner what he must say, or what would
be in the document that he must sign. In the document
Abed admitted to passing money from one man to another to be used for recruitment in the Popular Committees so members could continue writing on walls,
distributing the leaflets of Unified Leadership and dis-
rupting public security.

The confession also said: "Six months ago two congressmen from the United States came to my house,
asked me to show Jabalia camp and I agreed. . . . We
made a tour and they took photos. Later on they left. I
don't remember their names but I have their visiting
cards at home."

This struck an odd clang for the Americans he took
on tour and who stayed in his house were aides to congressmen, not themselves the legislators. Their two
cards were still in his house, in a drawer, for he always

kept such souvenirs: one belonged to Perry Plumart, office of Congressman Fortnay Stark, the other from Matthew Doss who worked for Congressman George E. Brown, Jr.

Perhaps the prisoner hoped to save himself by saying they were important congressmen, perhaps he thought this would send a signal to his friends when they saw the confession that he had been forced to invent.

Bill Warnock was deeply suspicious and notified a colleague in the Washington office of World Vision: ". . . The Officer taking the 'confession' works from notes prepared by the interrogators and returns the prisoner to the interrogator if he no longer confirms the material in his notes."

On March nineteenth, the indefatigable Mr. Warnock was told by Abed's lawyer that it would be helpful if he appeared in court. The prisoner's family and friends assembled outside the Gaza Central Military Court. Abed was expected to arrive by bus.

"We waited outside in the sun with many other families of Palestinians—ninety-five cases were scheduled for court meeting that day—from nine A.M. until three-thirty P.M. when Abed's case came up."

Inside the courtroom people struggled and shouted above the din. It was even difficult to be admitted. Mr. Warnock, a devout Episcopalian who was not easily discouraged, or intimidated, again reported to his American colleagues on how the day had gone.

After strong questioning by two soldiers on guard at the court, the lawyer and I persuaded them to let me, Abed's father and his brother, into the courtroom. Inside was near pandemonium. About 25 prisoners were led into the dock at once. The tiny visitors' gallery was crammed with 80 to 100 family members of the accused. Many other family members, including Abed's brother and mother, were not allowed in to witness the trials of their loved ones. The soldiers prevented the prisoners from speaking to their families, though occasionally some of the kinder soldiers allowed some limited interchange. This was interspersed by barked shouts and threats to the witnesses by soldiers, and some were forcibly ejected and even struck outside the courtroom. It was a distressing scene. I couldn't help noting the tragic similarities between the young prisoners in the dock and the young soldiers, some with flashes of humanity, charged with keeping order in the court. It reinforced my conviction that we must do all we can to speed the process of achieving peace with justice for both Israelis and Palestinians.

Charge sheets against prisoners were read, lawyers made brief presentations, arguments took place between judges and prosecutor, judges and lawyers, and each case was dealt with in what seemed to be summary fashion. Acquittals are practically unheard of, and no accusers appeared at any of the trials I witnessed.

Abed's lawyer had had no access to him since their last meeting in January. They had to hold a hasty, improvised shouting match across the row of prisoners in front of Abed, with many other lawyers trying to consult with their clients as well. The lawyer had no opportunity to really discuss alterna-

tives with Abed before he and all others were ordered to silence on entry of three judges.

It was not reassuring when Gideon Levy, an Israeli
journalist, published an interview, on January 5, 1990,
in the weekly magazine of the newspaper *Ha'aretz*, with
Shin Bet agents titled "The Best Years of Their Lives."
In the article the agents, who were not identified, referred to Shin Bet as Shabac. The agency's formal name
is Sherut Bitochan.

Mr. Warnock, horrified, sent on excerpts from the
piece to the Washington, D.C. office of World Vision.

Agent X says: "First of all, you should know that
this interrogation system isn't the Securitate or the
KGB. If a detainee died from blows, there is a
reasonable chance that it wasn't in the framework
of a Shabac investigation. A detainee passes
through a lot of stations before he reaches 'the
interrogation cellars' of Shabac. He passes through
the hands of noncombat units, whose soldiers are
the usual bestial level of army kitchen and ware-
house workers. They'll kill me for what I'm saying but I mean it. At the same time, I'm not
completely naive, and I wouldn't be surprised if
they also died during Shabac interrogations, but
this is exceptional.

"Once I brought a detainee to the administration, and a border policeman came by and gave him
a punch. . . . When we bring a prisoner to the
administration, every infected piece of scum jumps
on him. . . . Now, I'll tell you something psychoana-
lytical: Give the most enlightened and cultured

people the same authorization to open doors that Shabac has, and they'll have to have incredible spiritual strength not to fall into the attitude that they are above the law."

Agent Y is quoted as saying: "There is a problem with the Arabs, a mental problem. It's terrible what I'm saying, but they're basically different from Westerners—it's in the genetic structure. This sounds racist, but did you know that a Bedouin can't pass a polygraph because his moral level is completely different than yours. For him, to kill his sister is OK. He can say black is white, and it will come out true on the polygraph. It's possible that if you slap him, he'll tell the truth. A non-Arab has never been beaten by Shabac, to the best of my knowledge. Because people like you or me, there's no need to beat. . . . An Arab is different."

The American went on:

One can form one's own conclusions as to how much credence can be given to any "confession" gained at their hands. After the Israeli Government's Landau Commission discovered that Shin Bet agents have systematically lied under oath concerning interrogation techniques for the past 16 years, nonetheless it held they should be allowed to use "moderate physical force" and psychological pressure to obtain confessions. While the same report states there are "red lines" beyond which Shin Bet cannot go in interrogations, they have kept those "red lines" secret. Many ex-detainees have testified at length on the pervasive use of torture in

Israeli prisons. A thorough investigation of how
Abed's "confession" was obtained should be made
by an impartial authority.

By then the charge of buying ammunition was
dropped and another lesser charge reduced. The prosecutor asked for a minimum two-year sentence for Abed
despite the reduced charges and, at the request of the
lawyer, Mr. Warnock was invited by the judges to address the court. He did his best, saying that since Abed
worked sixty to eighty hours a week it was hard to understand how he could have done all the activities in the
charge sheet.

"I said that visitors from my organization, as well as
parliamentary and congressional groups had been very
impressed by the intelligent, balanced and articulate
presentations made by Abed on their meetings with
him," Mr. Warnock noted. One reason for choosing
Abed to meet such groups was his ability to speak English and the job he held. The young nurse spoke of the
suffering of Gazans and the cost of the occupation but
did not deliver a political analysis or ever attack the
Jewish state. Mr. Warnock knew full well that the court
knew of these meetings and somehow felt that this contact with foreigners, not any specific actions, was the
undoing of Abed Ajrami. On the lawyer's advice he did
not mention the irregularities in due process cited in a
letter about Abed's confession from Senator Mark Hat-
field, a member of the board of World Vision.

The sentencing came later: fifteen months' imprisonment plus either a fine equivalent to one thousand
dollars, or four additional months' imprisonment. Abed
and the lawyer were happy with the light sentence and

the Palestinian was sent back to Ansar III in the Negev desert where he is prisoner 23724. The prosecutor made known that he would press for an appeal to secure a longer sentence. No one guessed that he would succeed the next year.

It was an ordinary case except for those who loved or cared for Abed Ajrami and kept praying for him as there was nothing else to do once important people, and organizations, had been asked to inquire, or intercede. The sad family in Gaza prayed. In London, Dr. Swee, who put her Christian beliefs above all else even her own life, prayed. In Jerusalem a bishop prayed and in Washington, D.C. a few busy people prayed, too. And Abed, a Christian, must have prayed too during his interrogation for all men did. So many people remembered him with affection and respect and made up letters, as I did, that were never sent, calling on him to be strong. But like most Palestinians he was already stronger than we would ever manage to be.

At the end of December and in January of the new year nearly all the rooms in Marna House were empty and the books carried such a long way had been read and only whitened the long nights. They lay on the little table near the narrow bed: *Conversations with Primo Levi*, a new novel, *The Extras*, and Etty Hillsum's *Letters from Westerbork*. In the last postcard that Etty Hillsum threw out of the train that would take three days to reach Auschwitz, she wrote: "We left the camp singing, Father and Mother firmly and calmly, Mischa too."

At night I ate dinner alone, sometimes staring at the fading old framed photograph on a wall of the roses in the garden that Margaret Nassar had so loved. It was said that she even went to the British War Cemetery in Gaza for cuttings, perhaps convinced their roses came from England.

Sometimes even the Gazans felt claustrophobic if for reasons of money or lack of the required new ID card or fear of passing through military checkpoints they felt themselves pinned down. A few men had to escape for their lives depended on it, an alarm had been sounded, a warning whispered by one of their own that an arrest would soon be made. The escape took money and contacts and the insane will that the hunted must always summon.

There was the sea but the Israelis had their boats and searchlights. There was the border with Egypt but it was guarded with barbed wire and a watch tower and weapons. There was the open aboveground stream of sewage that had burst its limits in Tel Essultan in Rafah, the southernmost area on the Strip that faced Egypt. Some Palestinians escaped by creeping and wading through its waste, the rank slush.

"If you understand our lives this way is fitting," said a Palestinian high school teacher when we talked in his garden with its two orange trees. He said his own parents always thought the smell of the orange and lemon groves in Palestine kept people from falling ill.

It was always in Rafah where the Gazans would not permit themselves to be treated as weeds. The partisans were the population, no one was neutral. It was here where they flew the huge flag of Palestine, not the tiny one that hung from the wires in camps and other places on the Strip. No regard was given to the soldiers who

could see the flags a good distance away. The people
went about their business, the flags flapping, as if they
lived in a world of their own making and were not the
servants of anyone.

Their worse casualties in Rafah were always sent to
the town of Gaza. Only a week before a boy named
Omar with an eyeball like a raw red egg arrived in an
ambulance at the Eye Hospital, the only one. It was on
one floor, with thirty-five beds, a modern operating
room and a laser machine, an immaculate place with one
disadvantage. It was just above Gaza's only psychiatric
hospital, which had no psychiatrist on its staff, and
whose distraught male patients sometimes wandered
about the building or walked the grounds. There was
concern they might go up the stairs.

In the examining room of the Eye Hospital, Omar
lay, waiting for the surgeon who was in the mosque and
had to be summoned. He whimpered and shivered and
gave up hope, passing out again. His age was thirteen.
His hair was roughened by dried blood and there were
marks on the thin chest. Someone covered him with a
blanket and tried to clean him up without touching the
mess around the right eye whose socket looked so queer.

When his mother arrived from Rafah, leading other
members of the family, her sharp and big face a map of
trouble, she had a lot to say.

"During clashes in the camp the soldiers were running after boys and suspecting that one boy entered our
house they kicked in the door but found only me and
Omar. They began beating him right there inside the
house with the butt of their rifles. Oh yes I tried to stop
them when an officer slapped me. The three soldiers

kept on hitting Omar on the head, chest, and especially in the eye."

There were fourteen other children in the family but she would not leave the hospital and sat through the operation on a bench sometimes leaning on the wall not wanting to speak anymore. She stayed all that night with the child. After the surgery, the nurse who wanted the British textbook on ophthalmology said Omar had suffered a fracture of the right eye socket and lost two centimeters of skin from the beating but the cornea seemed okay. A skin graft had been done; vision would be restored, perhaps eighty percent.

The children were always being injured, never seen as innocent by most soldiers who were enraged by the sight of them. Possessed with such power the power possessed the Israelis. Not soldiers enduring long or intense periods of combat, since the Palestinians did not use weapons or fire upon them, the Israelis could not claim they were psychically altered or damaged by their short tours in Gaza. It was not Lebanon. What was revealed were not the usual symptoms of the soldier too long in combat, only a hatred so easily aroused and so deeply implanted, a madness of its own.

There was a last visit to Rafah in mid-January when the green, white and black flag with the red triangle hung over three streets. Wandering around, a friend of the Palestinian guide led us to a small workplace where two men at sewing machines were making lined children's parkas of Israeli material which they sold wholesale. Glad of a chance to stop and chat, the older man joked about his wife and said we should meet her, really she was something, a woman without fear that one. He again told a little story which the other man at the sewing machine liked hearing again. Besides they had almost finished the morning's work, their quota was always six parkas a day and sometimes they worked beyond the hour when Palestinians were supposed to stop. They had families to feed but did not love the intifada less.

It went like this: on Friday, December 9, 1989, soldiers in their neighborhood began looking for men to take down the large Palestinian flag hanging from the power lines. They came to the house of the tailor, who was at work, and cornered a thirty-two-year-old male cousin, able-bodied but considered dim-witted. The cousin heard the order. He thought. "No," he said, "I will not do it." Wanting to save the cousin, and fearing for her sons, the wife stepped forward, a volunteer. Five women stayed with her as she marched into the street, flanked by those friends.

At my insistence, the tailor cheerfully led us home so his forty-seven-year-old wife might speak for herself. A small, strong-looking woman with a face darkened by the sun, Fatmah had six children and was a little too busy to waste time. So she gave a factual account without embellishments and the proud husband listened with a small smile. On that Friday she found a pole and took down the piece of cloth as an officer and soldiers from the Givati Brigade watched.

What the obstinate woman did next was unforgivable to the men. Taking her time she neatly folded the flag, held it in her hands for a second and lowered her head to kiss it. Only then did she hand it over to the officer.

"A soldier said in Arabic 'God damn you,'" said
Fatmah. "Well, it's our right to kiss the flag." She
showed us how she had done it, the ancient sacred kiss,
the priest touching the altar with his lips.

Every Gazan knew the penalty for such an act so
Fatmah stood, frozen, awaiting the blow. It was useless
to run. She thought two of the soldiers were moving in
when the miracle happened. A U.N. van driving by
suddenly stopped and out stepped a bearded man, a
Refugee Affairs Officer from UNRWA, speaking English. He did not know what had taken place, he only
saw the soldiers bunching up, and the women standing
very still. Smiling, he said to the officer: "It seems you
have a problem. What can we do . . ." It was his job to
intervene in such incidents as diplomatically as possible,
the welfare of the refugees his concern.

Perhaps it helped that he did not look too Anglo-
Saxon, coming from a family of Armenian origin. He
was a thirty-nine-year-old industrial psychologist from
California named Fred Brauer but no one knew that
much when he so skillfully interfered. The soldiers were
stymied by the American with his agreeable, patient
manner so the women raced home. The little group
around her that day, as she gave her account, agreed that
this bearded stranger had been a blessing.

At Marna House that night there was no other guest
to hear how a woman honored the forbidden flag and
Alya was on the telephone. The garden, for all its sweetness, was too cold at night to sit outside.

The year sank to its end with more prayers, more
pleas for peace, more anger, more prayers, more criticism of the occupation and derision for those who as-

sailed it. The Anglican Archbishop of South Africa, Desmond Tutu, visited Jerusalem, only an hour from Gaza but as remote as Capetown or London, and said a prayer at a memorial, near the Dome of the Rock mosque, for the Palestinian victims of the Sabra and Shatila massacre in Lebanon. His presence worried and disturbed many Israelis, who were not grateful for his earlier remarks in the newspaper, *Ha'aretz:* "I am a black South African and if I were to change the names, a description of what is happening in Gaza and the West Bank could describe events in South Africa."

B'Tselem, the Israeli Information Center for Human Rights in the Occupied Territories, released its first annual report on human rights violations. Its editor Roni Talmor, speaking at the time of publication, said: "If we compare the first year of the intifada to its second with regards to human rights violations in the territories we can say: everything is the same, only more so. There were more people killed, more wounded, more house demolitions, more arrests, more administrative detainees, more places in detention centers, more days under curfew, more restrictions of movement, more limits on freedom of expression, more use of administrative punitive measures."

The Civil Administration was considered an arm of punishment and connected to all the punitive measures used by the security forces.

Deportations were ended. This happened only because the defense establishment "wants to expel immediately without giving the deportee time to petition the High Court of Justice, and the Justice Ministry does not permit this," the editor said. Because the Israeli military believed delayed deportations were ineffective, expulsion orders were no longer issued.

"When they stop hating us they will start to hate each other and that will be the end of it," a thirty-eight-year-old Gazan shoemaker said but it was not a prophecy, only what he needed to believe.

All the flags went up in Rafah, came down and were hoisted again as if no power on earth could prevent this. The woman who kissed the flag knew her own daughters would someday do what she had done. The old pain made them reckless and more persistent.

The third year of the intifada began. The Israeli reservists, in their endless rotations, were jubilant to leave Gaza and did not make known all that had happened when they were home once more. Then, in the summer of 1990, a fresh and diverse disaster startled many nations when, in the Persian Gulf, a tiny rich kingdom bloated with oil was quickly seized and swallowed by Iraq. The tragic contradictions came soon enough: old allies were new enemies, old enemies were quickly courted and won over. The Iraqi aggressor, once so favored that he was given billions of dollars in loans, was now compared to Hitler.

The peculiar new alliances and ruptures, the oratory from leaders who lacked the gift, the television film of American soldiers in the desert and pilots who could not see where sky, sand or sea began and ended, claimed all our attention. There were thousands of new hostages whose wives began to plead for their release and a multitude of foreign workers, suddenly penniless and stranded, fleeing occupied Kuwait. The United Nations was suddenly useful, even crucial. Everywhere people waited for war and some were hoping for it.

It was a discouraging time for those Israelis who, in the words of Camus, wanted to love their country and love justice. Many, who believed in the right of Palestinians to have their own nation, were repelled by their intense acclaim for an Iraqi despot.

In the Occupied Territories Palestinians did not feel forgotten because Saddam Hussein linked the withdrawal of his troops from Kuwait to an Israeli withdrawal from Gaza and the West Bank. The intifada, which seemed only a minor convulsion with ugly spasms now and then, could no longer be overlooked as the killings increased. Because no other Arab leader spoke so loudly, so harshly, on their behalf it was not surprising that he excited and impressed the Palestinians who for so long felt themselves betrayed and unprotected.

Not everyone believed in him. But in Gaza they knew how to wait, how not to give in to hopelessness. It was as the fisherman put it that summer day when he came home with the shrimp. If it meant two years or ten years before there was a Palestinian state that was all right.

"But it must come," he said. "We have to have this."

Epilogue, 1990

APRIL: Prime Minister Yitzhak Shamir rejects a United States plan for Israel-Palestinian talks and says that foreign governments are trying to force him to negotiate with the P.L.O. The issue is always what relationship Palestinian negotiators would have to the P.L.O.

A 1,000-page report sponsored by the Swedish Save the Children organization accuses Israeli soldiers of "using severe, indiscriminate and recurrent" violence against children in the Occupied Territories. "Nearly a fifth of the children were shot dead while at home or within ten meters of their home," the report said.

MAY: A new strategy on the part of Chairman Yasir Arafat of the P.L.O. moves him closer to Iraq's leader, *The New York Times* reports. Several thousand P.L.O. guerrillas, scattered in various Arab nations after their retreat from Lebanon, are ordered to relocate to Iraq. Fearing a new government of Yitzhak Shamir in Israel, and the possibility of a wave of Soviet Jews being resettled in the territories, Arafat suggests war may be imminent.

A prominent Israeli lawyer who for twenty-three years defended Palestinians closes her Jerusalem office in "disgust and despair," *The Washington Post* reports. Fifty-nine-year-old Felicia Langer says that justice cannot be obtained for Palestinians in the territories who need protection.

Seven miles south of Tel Aviv, an Israeli male civilian shoots and kills seven day laborers from Gaza and wounds seven. The deaths provoke violent reactions in the Occupied Territories and protests in Jordan. The Bush administration again says that peace talks are crucial to prevent such violence.

At an Arab summit meeting in Baghdad, called by Yasir Arafat, President Saddam Hussein says the U.S. bears major responsibility for the Israeli aggression directed at the Palestinian people. The month before, the Iraqi leader threatened to use chemical weapons in retaliation if Israel attacked Iraq.

Israeli forces foil guerrillas in two speedboats attempting to land on the coast of Israel to kill civilians. The raid was believed to be ordered by Abul Abbas, head of a small P.L.O. faction which hijacked the *Achille Lauro*. Arafat's refusal to condemn Abbas and this action leads to the suspension of U.S. talks with Palestinians.

JUNE: After a bitter struggle, the seventy-four-year-old Yitzhak Shamir forms a new government, the most conservative ever, whose policies alarm Arabs. A deepening hostility arises from Washington's veto of a United Nations Security Council resolution to send U.N. observers to the West Bank and Gaza and from

Washington's inability to press Israel harder toward a dialogue with the Palestinians under American and Egyptian sponsorship.

The Israeli government says Soviets would not be resettled beyond the Green Line, the demarcation between Israel and the occupied land.

Secretary of State James A. Baker 3d tells the Congress that the U.S. is weary of the foot-dragging of the Israelis to start talks in Cairo with Palestinian representatives of people in the Occupied Territories who would negotiate with Israel about self-rule. The peace plan was one introduced by Shamir himself more than a year earlier but which he did not intend to carry out.

J U L Y :   Saddam Hussein accuses Kuwait and the United Arab Emirates of flooding the oil market and driving prices down causing Iraq to lose oil revenues. Iraq also accuses Kuwait of stealing billions of dollars from the oil field that straddles their shared border. Kuwait officials claim that Iraq needs to dismiss its creditors, including Kuwait, to write off billions of dollars of debt from its eight-year war with Iran.

A U G U S T :   On the 2nd the Iraqi army invades Kuwait, whose wealth comes not only from oil but from international investments. The Emir and his family escape. On the 7th, to prevent Saudi Arabia from being menaced by Iraq the United States, asked for help by King Fahd, sends troops, planes and an armada of warships to Saudi Arabia where an international air, land and sea force will exist. It is the fastest military buildup in American history. A worldwide trade and financial embargo against Iraq is ordered by the United Nations Security Council. On the 17th, appearing on ABC's "Nightline" program, the Foreign Minister of Iraq says, "Iraq never had any intention to attack Saudi Arabia militarily. This has been used as a pretext in the region. . . ." On the 21st Iraq calls for talks on ending the Persian Gulf crisis but does not offer to withdraw from Kuwait. The White House refuses, saying that no talks are possible until Iraq unconditionally carries out the United Nations demand that it withdraw its forces. In *The New York Times* Thomas Friedman writes: "Bush Administration officials insist that for the United States and its allies to achieve their objectives President Hussein must not only retreat from Kuwait but he must do so in a manner that leaves no suggestion that Iraq gained from its invasion. Officials say he must not only be defeated, he must be seen as defeated by everyone in the Arab world."

More than half a million foreigners, who worked in Kuwait, flee by crossing into Jordan. Tens of thousands of them are trapped in a no-man's-land between the Iraqi and Jordanian frontiers unable to return to their own countries.

On the 22nd the U.S. summons 40,000 reservists to support the trooplift, the first call-up since the 1968 Tet Offensive in Vietnam.

President Hussein decides to let foreign women and children leave Iraq. Foreign males become hostages.

SEPTEMBER: Meeting in Finland, President Bush and President Mikhail Gorbachev issue a joint pledge to reverse Iraq's conquest of Kuwait, a historic political collaboration.

The vast number of Soviet immigrants arriving in Israel, expected to exceed 150,000 for the year, causes an acute shortage and resentment of the preferential treatment given the newcomers.

President Hafez Assad of Syria agrees to send troops to Saudi Arabia and aligns himself with President Bush's position that there must be no linkage between a settlement of the Gulf con-

flict and a settlement of the Arab-Israel conflict as called for by
Saddam Hussein.

Over 150,000 U.S. troops are in the Gulf but the ceiling is
higher. Nine hundred American men are still in Iraq and occupied Kuwait.

The support given to Iraq by Yasir Arafat and senior P.L.O.
leaders causes deep disruptions and confusion in the Arab world.
The New York Times reports that the P.L.O. has received ten
billion dollars from Kuwait, Saudi Arabia and the United Arab
Emirates, who will not easily overlook such a breach of loyalty.

Palestinian support for Saddam Hussein, perceived as a new
ally, is intense. George Habash, head of the Popular Front for the
Liberation of Palestine, and Nayef Hawatmeh, head of the Democratic Front for the Liberation of Palestine, both acknowledge,
according to a *New York Times* story, that Palestinian support for
Iraq has set back their attempts to gain wider support for their
cause.

The support of sympathetic Israelis and other foreigners for
the intifada diminishes as the Gulf crisis grows more dangerous.
An article in *Ha'aretz*, the Israeli newspaper, written by Yossi
Sarid, a member of parliament who has long advocated Palestinian self-determination, expresses a new and widely felt bitter-
ness and disgust with the Palestinian alliance with Iraq. *The Wall
Street Journal* gives a translation of the comments of Mr. Sarid,
whose Citizen's Rights Party has supported the Palestinians.

"If it is permissible to support Saddam Hussein—who murdered tens of thousands of 'regime opponents' without blinking
an eyelid, who gassed Kurds, men, women and children, then
perhaps it is not too bad to support the policy of Mr. Shamir, Mr.
Sharon and Mr. Rabin," he wrote.

"Had I supported the establishment of a Palestinian state

only because the Palestinians deserved such a state I would now withdraw that support," Mr. Sarid said. "However I continue to demand their right for self-determination and an independent state because it is my right to rid myself of the occupation and its evil influence. The Palestinians perhaps deserve the occupation but we Israelis do not. . . ."

An Israeli army officer is burned to death inside his car when he drives into the refugee district of Bureij in the Gaza Strip. After his vehicle hits a donkey cart, injuring two boys, a crowd of Palestinians stones and sets fire to the vehicle. Authorities say the officer was looking for his unit but Gazans refute this. The murder provokes reprisals, and a curfew for Bureij of more than six days.

The New York Times reports that an increasing number of Israelis are moving to the West Bank and Gaza. Israel only pledged not to send the Soviet immigrants to the territories and East Jerusalem.

The Soviet Foreign Minister, in a speech at the U.N. General Assembly, warns President Hussein that a war in the Persian Gulf may be imminent if his troops are not pulled out of Kuwait.

Marc Humbert of the Associated Press reports that New York governor Mario Cuomo said to the Rochester Chamber of Commerce: "Now you're on the edge of war because of oil. Be honest—who cares about the Kuwaiti royalty. . . . You're there for oil. You know it and I know it. And we shouldn't be there for oil." More attention should be devoted to energy sources that could replace oil, he said.

The President's National Security Advisor said after meeting with the Emir of Kuwait that the "systematic destruction" of Kuwait was shortening the time that the U.S. could wait for economic sanctions to force the Iraqis out of Kuwait.

An editorial in *The New York Times*, complaining about the

unfair costs of Operation Desert Shield, says, "And even if there is no fighting, the U.S. already finds itself paying twice, once to defend Iraq's neighbors and again for oil at twice the July price. Saudi Arabia, whose oil profits are expected to jump by $50 billion a year, has pledged $12 billion to reimburse Washington for its gulf-related military operations and help defray the impact of the embargo on its poor neighbors. But that doesn't begin to cover the bill."

The presence of the United States forces on the land of "the state which is the custodian of the two holiest shrines of Islam must be terminated within the shortest possible period of time," King Hussein of Jordan says in a television interview on Cable News Network, "lest it result in incalculably grave consequences for Arabs and Muslims the world over for generations to come." Mecca and Medina are the holy sites in southwestern Saudi Arabia.

OCTOBER: *The Wall Street Journal* reports on the findings of members of the German Parliament on the German role in arming Iraq. Economics Minister Helmut Haussmann reveals that German companies were involved in virtually every major Iraq weapons program. "From poison gas plants to rocket factories, from cannon forges to the nuclear sector . . . the danger has already been spread," he said. Criminal proceedings start against twenty-five companies.

No force should be used in the Persian Gulf, the Chief of the Soviet Staff said in an interview with writers and editors of *The New York Times.* Stressing the need for United Nations approval for any attack by the United States and other nations opposed to the Iraqi invasion of Kuwait, the top Soviet General said economic sanctions were working.

In an address to the General Assembly at the U.N. the

Foreign Minister of Saudi Arabia urges Iraq to relinquish Kuwait
to bolster the right of Palestinians to claim a homeland in the
territories occupied by Israel. The Saudi commitment toward the
Palestinian people, the Minister said, "was not born today nor
yesterday, it was born with the first heartbeat of the cause." His
remarks held a warning to the P.L.O. and Palestinians that they
were hurting their own struggle if they supported the Iraqi annexation of Kuwait.

After receiving American pledges for $400 million in loan
guarantees to pay for Soviet immigrant housing Foreign Minister
David Levy said, in Jerusalem, when asked about the U.S. requirement that Israel promise that the money not be used for new
settlements in Gaza and the West Bank: "Ask what they demanded and what they got. The demands they were making were
unacceptable and were rejected out of hand . . ."

By pushing trade sanctions through the Security Council
and starting the military buildup in the Gulf, the Foreign Minister of Iraq claims, the United States and its allies prevented Arab
countries from resolving the crisis among themselves. In the
speech read for him before the General Assembly of the U.N. the
Minister repeats Iraq's claim that Kuwait is an artificial nation
created by Britain out of its territory in 1913. Arabs at the United
Nations start a new campaign to equate the Gulf crisis with the
Palestinian question.

The Defense Minister of Saudi Arabia says Israel must stay
out of the Gulf crisis and that if Israel and Saudi Arabia find
themselves at war with Iraq Saudi Arabia would fight alone and
not allow Israel to come to its defense.

Clyde Farnsworth in *The New York Times* reports on the
system by which aid is given to Israel. He writes: "Sometime
before October 30 the Treasury will write a check to Israel for
$1.2 billion. The money, almost half of the $3 billion in economic

and military aid that the United States gives Israel every year, will be quietly deposited in the Federal Reserve Bank of New York and immediately start earning interest at about 8 percent." The remaining amount goes to the Pentagon and a trust fund that pays for F-15s, Stinger Missiles, TOW antitank missiles, Bradley fighting vehicles and other goods purchased from American military contractors. "This system, used only for Israel, opens the spigot for millions of dollars of interest, in effect, added aid that does not go through the appropriations process," he wrote. Special favors for Israel have been built into foreign-assistance laws in recognition of close ties between the two countries.

U.S. soldiers in Saudi Arabia working an eight-to-twelve-hour day in the summer heat require two or three gallons of water a day, and during conditions of continuous battle might need to drink as much as six gallons a day, *The Washington Post Health* magazine reports.

President Saddam Hussein threatens to attack oil fields in Saudi Arabia, other Arab countries and Israel if economic sanctions imposed by the United Nations "strangle" Iraq, *The New York Times* reports. Blaming the United States for the sanctions, the statement of President Hussein also says the penalties had been imposed "in a way that exceeds all humanitarian limits."

On the 8th, twenty-one Palestinians are shot to death by the paramilitary Israeli police in Jerusalem, near Al Aksa Mosque, in the deadliest incident since the intifada began in December 1987. The two sides give differing accounts of the tragedy in which more than one hundred Palestinians were injured. The Palestinians assembled in the mosque compound, they said, after being told that a Jewish group, the Temple Mount Faithful, planned to enter the compound to lay a symbolic cornerstone near the mosques for a new Jewish temple. The Al Aksa Mosque and another, the Dome of the Rock, twelve-hundred-year-old

Muslim shrines, are where the biblical Jewish temples once stood.

Hurling stones, rocks and bottles down at the Jewish worshipers below praying at the Western Wall, injuring eleven people but not seriously, the Palestinians greatly outnumber the police. When more police arrive, tear gas is used, then rubber bullets and live ammunition. The shooting goes on for thirty to forty minutes.

On the 9th, Hugh Carnegy in the *Financial Times* says: "Of all the people hearing the news from Jerusalem yesterday, President George Bush and his small circle of advisers steering U.S. policy in the Gulf must surely have been among those who felt the deepest shock and foreboding. Israel's much remarked upon 'low profile' in the Gulf crisis has been somewhat exaggerated. . . . But yesterday's killings in Jerusalem abruptly dispelled any chance of Israel and the Palestinian issue remaining out of the Gulf picture."

President Bush, hoping to maintain the support of Arab countries in the U.S.-led coalition against Iraq, asks the United Nations Security Council to approve a resolution condemning Israel for excessive use of force in killing Palestinians in Jerusalem. Resentment runs high among Israeli officials for this action.

Despite the worldwide condemnation, the Israeli government continues to blame the Palestinians for the killings in the Old City of Jerusalem and appoints its own commission to investigate the deaths.

Sporadic clashes take place in the West Bank and Gaza where the Jerusalem victims are mourned.

A *Wall Street Journal* editorial says: "The latest deadly violence in Jerusalem is part of the mounting cost of U.S. indecision in the Persian Gulf. Yasir Arafat, a close ally of Saddam Hussein, has been doing what he can to shift the world's attention from Saddam to Israel. . . . From the first days of the Iraqi conflict, there has been a consensus that one of Saddam's few hopes lay in dragging Israel into the conflict."

The Security Council unanimously passes a resolution condemning the violence in Jerusalem but in language less harsh than many delegates wished but which the U.S. wanted. Israeli security forces are criticized but the Security Council fails to obtain a clear mandate to protect Palestinians under Israeli occupation which the P.L.O. pressed for.

In an article investigating the Jerusalem deaths, Joel Brinkley of *The New York Times* writes that his inquiry "shows that both sides have been offering incomplete and partly inaccurate accounts." The violence began when Palestinians threw stones at police on guard at the edge of the Western Wall. The police were vastly understaffed and had to retreat when large numbers of Palestinians advanced toward them. Then the Palestinians "rained stones onto Jews praying at the Western Wall below. . . ." When the police returned in larger numbers automatic weapons were used on crowds of Palestinians. The chief cleric at Al Aksa Mosque said during Friday prayers, attended by 20,000 people, he had called on Muslims to protect the mosque from the Jewish extremist group who wants to build a new temple on the site where Herod's Temple stood almost two thousand years ago. The Israeli government does not sanction the demolition of mosques. A report by B'Tselem, the respected Israeli human rights organization, said it did not discover any preparations for violent action as Israelis had claimed. According to B'Tselem's investigation the shooting began after the police themselves no longer faced any significant threat to their lives. The article quoted the report which said: "If there were stages in which concrete mortal danger existed this was a brief stage at the beginning of the riot" before live ammunition was used.

Relations between the United States and Israel are deeply

strained. On the fifteenth a committee of the Israeli cabinet decides to encourage an increase in the settlement of Soviet Jews in Jerusalem's annexed eastern section. *The New York Times* reports that this is a clear and defiant response to the American vote to send a U.N. delegation to Jerusalem to investigate the killings which Israel refuses to accept. Israelis see the delegation as a challenge to their sovereignty over Jerusalem.

Thomas Friedman in *The New York Times* writes: "Administration officials said that what is at stake now is not simply another difference of opinion between Washington and Jerusalem over the Israeli-Palestinian peace process, but the United States's strategy for dealing with Iraq which hinges on keeping an Arab and international coalition focused on rolling back the Iraqi invasion of Kuwait."

American Jewish organizations have mixed reactions to Israel's refusal to assist the U.N. mission to investigate the deaths in Jerusalem.

In an Op-Ed page article in *The Washington Post*, Judith Caesar, an American who taught English for three years at a university in Saudi Arabia, writes of growing resentment there against the Saudi royal family and the American military presence. In order to thwart Saudi censors, Saudi opinions are circulated on cassette tapes. On one widely circulated tape, a Saudi academic says that "the animosity between Islam and the West is a matter of fact and will continue. Therefore, it is wrong that such Westerners be invited to defend us."

In an interview with Judith Miller of *The New York Times*, King Hussein of Jordan, who has met with fifteen leaders in his efforts to achieve peace, says if war comes it will be partly because of a failure by President Bush and other Western leaders to respond in time to signals from the Iraqi leader that he was ready to withdraw from most of the occupied territory in Kuwait. "The

King argued . . . that the Iraqi invasion of Kuwait could have been prevented through astute Arab diplomacy, and that American forces would not have been needed if the Arabs had enough time to resolve the problems themselves," the story said.

The Washington Post reports that soaring oil prices have dealt "a double blow to the U.S. economy, worsening the country's inflation rate and increasing its trade deficit, the government reported yesterday." The increased cost of oil, triggered by Iraq's invasion of Kuwait, was reflected in the Labor Department's consumer price index for September which put the annual rate of inflation at 9.5 percent, about double last year's rate.

On the 18th the Associated Press reports Israeli troops shot and wounded thirty-five Palestinians in seven hours of clashes in the center of the Rafah refugee camp in Gaza after soldiers raised an Israeli flag in the center of the camp. Reuter's reports fifty-five wounded in the biggest clash since the October 8th killings in Jerusalem. It is the thirty-seventh month of the intifada. Israeli troops said the flag was raised over a new observation post. Twenty-six Palestinian youths were taken to a hospital with bullet wounds, two were shot in the head.

The Israeli Foreign Minister David Levy retracts a commitment made to Secretary of State James Baker 3d, according to *The New York Times,* that Israel would not settle more Soviet immigrants in East Jerusalem. But in a letter saying this he pledged that the costs of housing Soviet Jews or other immigrants here would not be financed with the $400 million in loans from the United States. To secure the loans Mr. Levy wrote to Mr. Baker that Israel "would not direct or settle immigrants beyond the green line," a reference to the armistice border separating Israel from the West Bank and East Jerusalem which remains largely Arab. Israel captured those territories in the 1967 war, then immediately annexed East Jerusalem and declared the united city its capital. In his newest letter, made available to reporters, Mr. Levy declared that Israel was under "no obligation—directly or indirectly—not to build in Jerusalem, or to limit buildings in Jerusalem, or in any other place," referring to the West Bank and Gaza.

On the 21st a Palestinian construction worker stabs to death three Israelis early in the morning in a quiet residential Jewish neighborhood in West Jerusalem in revenge for the deaths on October 8th. The assailant, who was shot and captured, acted on his own. Avi Pazner, spokesman for Prime Minister Yitzhak Shamir, said these killings were "the result of an atmosphere of incitement generated by the unjustified condemnation of Israel by the United Nations Security Council." The youngest victim was an eighteen-year-old female soldier, unarmed. A member of the Knesset and the Citizen's Rights Movement, Dedi Zucker said on the radio: "We have climbed in the last couple of months to a new stage of brutalization." Mayor Teddy Kollek, long an advocate of coexistence in Jerusalem, said the rage of Jewish crowds who attacked Arabs later that day was "justified."

After mounting violence—the stabbings of two Israeli women soldiers by an Arab, the shooting of three Gazans by Jewish civilians in a car, an attack by a Palestinian who beat two Jewish men with a sledgehammer—the Israeli government seals off the West Bank and Gaza Strip forbidding 1.8 million Palestinians to enter Israel. Hamas instructs Muslims in a leaflet to kill Jews.

An official Israeli commission investigating the killings in Jerusalem on October 8th supports the government's version, including the charges that Palestinians provoked the violence and that police gunfire was justified. Palestinian groups, revising the total given earlier, now give the number of dead as eighteen. The commission is criticized in Israel for relying almost exclusively on accounts by police.

The Persian Gulf drives United States–Israel relations to a historic ebb, *The Washington Post* reports.

Thousands rally in sixteen United States cities to protest American intervention in the Persian Gulf and rallies are also held in other countries. The protests are small.

In Los Angeles Secretary of State James Baker accuses the Iraqi government of "making political and economic war" on U.S. citizens held hostage in Iraq and Kuwait. He denounces the treatment of the one hundred Americans held as "human shields."

In *The Wall Street Journal* Tony Horwitz reports that after three months of U.N. trade sanctions "Iraq is a curious mixture of surface plenty and underlying shortage." The intensified pillage of Kuwait, rampant smuggling and nursing of vital supplies are enabling Iraq to survive. The reporter writes "there are few signs that the embargo is hitting hard enough to break Iraq's will."

NOVEMBER: In Riyadh, Saudi Arabia, the commander of the American forces, General H. Norman Schwarzkopf, says that his troops could obliterate Iraq but cautions that the total destruction of that country might "not be in the interest of the long-term balance of power in the region."

In a speech in Baghdad, Saddam Hussein declares that the Americans will be defeated no matter how many they are. He rejects again the approach suggested by President Bush that Iraq's demands for Israel's withdrawal from occupied Arab lands be addressed after an Iraqi pullout from Kuwait. "They shouldn't expect to placate us with promises to solve the Gulf crisis first and then the Palestinian problem." The Iraqi leader, according to a *New York Times* story, also said: "The battle is not over what happened on August 2nd. The battle now is over the Palestinian issue."

The Financial Times reports violence in the Gaza Strip on November 3rd and 4th as Palestinians demonstrate over a man's death in prison. The Israeli military says he committed suicide. Gazans suspect he died under interrogation and the newspaper reports that "thousands took to the streets to protest."

The Philadelphia Inquirer reports that the nonaligned nations of the U.N. Security Council request an urgent council meeting to discuss the violence in Gaza but the P.L.O. request for a U.N. observer force to monitor treatments of Palestinians in the Occupied Territories is thwarted.

On the 8th President Bush orders more than 150,000 additional U.S. ground, sea and air forces to the Persian Gulf area to increase the pressure on Iraq. With the new reinforcements the military deployment becomes the largest since the Vietnam War and changes the American mission from "defensive" to "offensive." It is expected that an offensive against Iraqi troops will be launched in 1991.

Total U.S. strengths for Operation Desert Shield will now reach almost 400,000 by January 1991.

Among the critics of the buildup are Senator Daniel Patrick Moynihan (Democrat, New York), who wants a more genuine effort to determine if economic sanctions would work. On ABC's television program "Good Morning America," Senator Moynihan says of the President: "He will wreck our military; he will wreck his administration and he'll spoil a chance to get a collective security system working. It breaks your heart."

Iraq sends 250,000 more troops to bolster its army in occupied Kuwait and nearby areas of southern Iraq.

Defense Secretary Richard Cheney announces that the Pentagon is no longer planning to rotate troops through Saudi Arabia and that the American forces already in the Persian Gulf area, or en route, will remain for the duration of the crisis. Earlier plans to rotate troops every six to eight months are now scrapped. *The New York Times* says: "The decision not to rotate troops could add to the pressure to bring the crisis to a conclusion soon, before troop morale deteriorates and the international coalition against Iraq weakens, which is something the administration fears."

In a speech opening the Jordanian Parliament King Hussein, a longtime ally and friend of the United States and other Western nations during his thirty-eight-year reign, once more calls for the removal of Western troops from Saudi Arabia. Attacking the Bush administration without naming it the King says: "Their actual goals stem from their desire to control our destiny and the Arab nations' resources." The monarch also says that it is hypocritical to try to uphold international law in the Persian Gulf while ignoring the plight of the Palestinians under Israeli occupation.

Nearly 150,000 Iraqi Army reservists must report for duty in occupied Kuwait.

Iraq offers to release all remaining foreign hostages in groups starting December 25th and continuing through March 25th "unless something should occur to disturb the atmosphere of peace." The announcement, reported by the Iraqi News Agency, seems timed to precede President Bush's Thanksgiving visit to the American troops in Saudi Arabia. U.S. and British officials dismiss the offer as more "cynical manipulation" of the 2,000 foreigners believed held, or trapped, in Iraq and Kuwait. The end date, March 25th, would fall near the beginning of the Muslim holy month of Ramadan.

The Senate Armed Services Committee starts hearings on

the Persian Gulf Crisis. The chairman of the panel, Senator Sam Nunn, once again questions the need for rushing into war.

President George Bush is widely criticized in the press and on television for not more clearly stating American goals in the Persian Gulf.

On November 27th *The New York Times* runs a table of the numbers of foreigners who were in Iraq and Kuwait before the August 2nd invasion and the numbers of men who still remain. More than 900,000 of an estimated three million foreigners of forty-two different nationalities have left, according to State Department and embassy registrations. Hundreds of Americans, Britons and Japanese are being held in Iraq and Kuwait as "human shields" at an estimated thirty strategic targets, the *Times* says. Up to 2,000 Westerners, including about 600 Americans, are hiding out in Kuwait.

The table indicates that of 3,500 Americans it appears there are still 930 still in these countries.

Philip Shenon of *The New York Times* reports from Baghdad that the city has "come to resemble a bazaar, this pleading and wheedling and haggling for the release of a hostage." Former heads of state from Europe, the President of Austria, a former prime minister of Japan, members of the British and Canadian Parliaments and Muhammad Ali, the former heavyweight boxing champion who converted to Islam, are among those who have been allowed to take out hostages from their own countries. The visits, highly controversial, are criticized as giving support to Saddam Hussein. "I basically believe that these people are playing into the propaganda game that Iraq is holding here," said Joseph C. Wilson 4th, the deputy chief of mission at the United States Embassy and the highest ranking American diplomat remaining in Baghdad. Families of detained Americans arrive in Baghdad to secure the release of a relative and are successful.

The Bush administration is urged not to rush into war and to give economic sanctions a year or more to take effect by two former chairmen of the Joint Chiefs of staff who address the Senate Armed Services Committee. Admiral William J. Crowe, Jr., says: "If in fact sanctions will work in twelve to eighteen months instead of six months, the trade-off of avoiding war with its attendant sacrifices and uncertainties would, in my view, be worth it."

By a vote of 12 to 2, the United Nations Security Council on November 29th authorizes the United States and its allies to expel Iraq from Kuwait by force if President Saddam Hussein does not withdraw his forces by January 15th. In a speech delivered hours before the vote the Iraqi leader said his nation was ready for war against the Americans. *The New York Times* reports that in a speech to students Saddam Hussein says: "If war breaks out we will fight in a way that will make all Arabs and Muslims proud. We are determined not to kneel down to injustice."

In a surprise announcement November 30th President Bush says he has asked the Secretary of State to go to Baghdad before January 15th to meet with the Iraqi leader. In a news conference Bush says the Baker mission reflects his desire "to go the extra mile." The Iraqi foreign minister is invited to Washington for consultations. The president discloses that the isolated U.S. Embassy in Kuwait was given fruits and cigarettes by Iraqis. He says too that he sees no need to reinstitute the draft.

DECEMBER: Lawmakers in Washington are pleased and relieved. A news analysis in *The Washington Post* says: "President Bush's abrupt turn-around in offering a high-level diplomatic exchange with Iraq is designed to head off criticism at home and abroad that he has not yet tested every avenue for a peaceful settlement of the Persian Gulf crisis, administration officials admit."

The Iraqi government accepts the American offer of direct talks. *The Washington Post* reports Iraqi insistence that the Palestine problem must be discussed in any dialogue.

In an interview with French journalists President Saddam Hussein says the chances of peace are "fifty-fifty."

Defense Secretary Dick Cheney tells Congress military action is the only way to force Iraq out of Kuwait. Conflicting opinions about the effectiveness of sanctions abound in the capitol.

On December 6th Saddam Hussein announces that all foreigners held in Iraq and Kuwait since the invasion are now free to go home. This new policy means their departures are imminent.

Prince Hussein of Jordan, after a meeting with the Iraqi leader, claims he is wholly convinced that Iraq will not leave Kuwait until the Palestinian problem is solved.

The U.S. Embassy in Kuwait, kept open and a sanctuary for Americans during the Iraqi occupation, is to be vacated once U.S. citizens are evacuated.

A U.N. Security Council resolution calls for measures to protect Palestinians in the territories and, under certain circumstances, the convening of an international conference to resolve the Arab-Israel conflict. The Bush administration, unwilling to use its veto for fear of alienating its Arab allies, postpones action on the resolution.

Claiming his schedule is too busy, Saddam Hussein says he cannot see Secretary of State Baker until January 12th. President Bush, angered, replies that he has offered the Iraqi any one of fifteen dates for the meeting in December and early January and that this is a maneuver to delay withdrawal by January 15th from Kuwait.

Secretary of State Baker says sanctions alone will not work and so does CIA director William Webster.

On December 13th the last American-sponsored flight takes off with Americans held in Iraq and Kuwait, and others.

Bickering grows heated between Washington and Baghdad about the dates for the meeting.

In Brussels, addressing NATO allies, Secretary of State Baker says he expects a ploy by Saddam Hussein—perhaps a partial withdrawal from Kuwait—before the January 15th deadline and that partial solutions are unacceptable.

The Israeli Defense Forces begin deploying hidden snipers along the highways in the West Bank to shoot, using live ammunition, any Palestinians stoning Israeli cars. In the Parliamentary debate a critic calls it "a monstrous order."

Deportations of Palestinians begin again in the Occupied Territories. The measure is used to prevent more stabbings of Israelis. Twenty have been killed this way, according to *The New York Times*. On December 15th four Palestinians believed members of Hamas, the Islamic Resistance Movement, are deported. A State Department spokesman protests, saying it is a violation of the Fourth Geneva Convention "as it pertains to the treatment of inhabitants of occupied territories," AP reports. Deportations were stopped in 1989 because of American, and international, protests.

In an attempt to crack down on Palestinians who might be members of Hamas the Israeli military sweeps through the West Bank and Gaza arresting 600. It is not reported how members of Hamas can be identified by the Israelis since lists are not kept.

The Israeli military orders the closure of 260 schools in Gaza and the Strip for an indefinite period of time. *The New York Times* gives 762 as the number of Palestinians killed since the intifada began on December 9, 1987, a number considered too low by Gazans.

On December 20th the United States finally votes in the U.N. Security Council for the United Nations to monitor the safety of Palestinians in the Occupied Territories. The new resolution refers to the lands occupied by Israel since 1967 as "Palestinian Territories."

On December 29th Israeli troops shoot and kill four men and wound more than 125 demonstrators in the Rafah and Khan Younis refugee camps in the Gaza Strip. After the first deaths in Rafah tens of thousands of Palestinians began demonstrations.